CLOSING TIME

Lockdown Reflections on a "Pubscrawling" Past

Closing Time

Lockdown Reflections on a "Pubscrawling" Past

Chris Arnot

This edition published 2021 by:
Takahe Publishing Ltd.
Registered Office:
77 Earlsdon Street, Coventry CV5 6EL

Copyright © Chris Arnot 2021

ISBN 978-1-908837-23-3

The moral rights of the author have been asserted.

All rights reserved. This publication may not be reproduced, stored in a retrieval system or transmitted, in any form or by any means, electronic, mechanical, photocopying, recording or otherwise, without the prior permission of the publishers.

Cover image courtesy of Pixabay

TAKAHE PUBLISHING LTD. 2021

*Cheers to the characters
who have kept me entertained
in pubs here, there and everywhere.*

Acknowledgements

Writing this book during lockdown meant that I couldn't revisit the many pubs that I've mentioned, for obvious reasons. Nor could I get hold of too many licensees on the phone. Two exceptions were Jackie Willacy at the Case is Altered in rural Warwickshire and Amanda Wilkinson at Hale's Bar in Harrogate. Thanks to them for sending me pictures of two much-treasured pubs. Thanks also to good friends whom I've occasionally turned to in order to jog my memory, rekindle stories from their past and mine, or to supply me with information or photographs. They are, in no particular order:

Graham Coster, Allister Craddock, Chris Holmes, John Holmes, John Hess, Patrick Freestone, John Middleton, Bruce Walker, Fred Luckett and Peter Walters.

Much gratitude to Keith Miller for commissioning so many Pint to Pint columns for the *Sunday Telegraph* and to Matthew Fort making space for my Pub of the Month column in *Guardian Weekend* back in the 1990s.

Also thanks to my wife Jackie for her steadfast support.

Humble apologies to anybody that I've forgotten.

- And I haven't forgotten Andrea Collins of the Bat and Ball in Hambledon, Dan Salmon from the Tafarn Sinc in Maenclochog and James Woolard from the Royal Oak near London Bridge, all of whom sent me pictures of their pubs once they were open for outside supping.

Contents

–	Introduction	1
1.	Landladies with Staying Power	9
2.	Redoubtable Landlords	25
3.	Where it All Started	39
4.	To London via Lancaster	55
5.	Goose Fair Peas and a Pint of "Shippo's"	71
6.	Batches and Bass in the City of Culture[s]	89
7.	Cricketing Pubs and the Tales Spun Around Them	119
–	Bibliography	133
–	Biography	135

Introduction

The French have long considered themselves *supérieur* in matters of food and drink. But I've occasionally detected an element of envy from across the Channel for one longstanding British source of refreshment.

"When you have lost your inns, drown your empty selves – for you will have lost the last of England," the philosopher Hilaire Belloc wrote in 1912. And rather more recently, when a French friend of friends of ours came from Paris on a visit with his father, they asked to be taken on a tour around some "typical" English pubs. Country pubs, preferably. A mini-bus was duly hired and we set forth into the wilds of Warwickshire with Claude and Georges.

I have two abiding memories of that evening. One was being in The Case is Altered at Five Ways – an ale-house down a rustic lane not far from the junctions of modern motorways and ancient canals.

The Case has altered little

Closing Time

The pub was originally called The Case. Until the mid 18th century, that is, when the landlord applied for a spirit licence and was declined on the basis that the premises were too small. Result: an extension into the cottage next door, spirit licence granted and name changed. The Case had been altered very little since, it seemed.

Nearly two and a half centuries later, beer was still served straight from the cask. However, it was no longer brewed by Lucas, Blackwell and Arkwright of Leamington Spa, despite an advertisement for their brews still dominating one wall. They had been taken over by Ansell's in 1928.

There was at least one open fire in the main bar. Plus some ancient, leather-bound settles. In the snug was a bar-billiards table. Balls were accessible only by feeding an old-fashioned sixpence into the slot. And to get one of those "tanners" you had to ask at the bar. After all, currency had been decimalised over twenty years previously.

* * * *

My other abiding memory of that evening of cross-Channel camaraderie was reaching the Shoulder of Mutton in Stretton-on-Dunsmore just before last orders. The pub was a strange mixture of the 1840s and the 1950s. Beer was propelled from barrel to glass via handpumps that looked as though they were made of Bakelite of the sort that might once have encased an early transistor radio broadcasting the Light Programme or the Home Service.

There was also a piano that could have predated the invention of the "wireless". It came to life now and again under the gnarled fingers of an octogenarian church organist peering through horn-rimmed specs at yellowing sheet music.

No piano tonight, mind you. There had been a darts match. Or possibly a shooting match. The Shoulder was one of very few pubs harbouring an air-rifle range. Darters or shooters were now tucking

Introduction

into beef dripping spread on bread that had been toasted, or at least warmed slightly, on an open fire that didn't so much roar as smoulder.

I've never forgotten watching two bemused French faces when our visitors were finally offered a slice to sample.

"Qu'est-ce que sais?" queried Claude.

"Je ne sais quoi," shrugged Georges.

Neither seemed inclined to sample more than a mouthful. Just as well, perhaps. The combination of beef fat and salt is not a recipe for a healthy heart.

The Shoulder of Mutton where beef dripping was once on offer

There'll always be a place in my heart, however, for the Shoulder of Mutton as it was it those days. The licensee was a genial gent called Paul Whitby. His widowed mother had been a formidable matron who demanded that customers left the premises no later than ten minutes after closing time. And she was not a woman to argue with. When she died, her body was laid out in the back parlour and the same regulars filed past reverentially.

The pub that she passed on to her son remained as it had always been. Until, that is, he moved on and it became a much more conventional hostelry serving food far fancier (and healthier) than beef dripping on toast.

But that evening of Anglo-French camaraderie in Five Ways and Stretton had rekindled my affection for eccentric alehouses. They were already becoming something of an endangered species in the last decade of the twentieth century. Luckily, I was able to convince the then food and drink editor of *The Guardian*, Matthew Fort, that there was some entertaining copy to be had. I was duly rewarded with the Pub of the Month column in that esteemed organ's Weekend supplement. The research required would take me all over England and, occasionally, beyond the borders into Wales and Scotland.

* * * *

Having dug out some dog-eared cuttings from the ancient filing cabinet in my office, I came across what may well have been my first piece for *Guardian Weekend*. The date was September 28, 1991, and it evidently preceded *Pub of the Month*. Went under the heading of "Eating Out" – a title usually reserved for Matthew himself, an eminent restaurant reviewer who could analyse the contents of cuisine dreamed up by top chefs in kitchens serving the poshest of London dining rooms.

My contribution to *Eating Out* was somewhat more downmarket. It was written after a visit to the buffet bar on Stalybridge Station (one stop out of Manchester Piccadilly on the Newcastle line) where the *pièce de résistance* was black peas served in a plastic cup and scooped up with a teaspoon. Alternatively, you could have them sloshed over a meat and potato pie. That would have set you back all of £1.30.

Introduction

It won't surprise you to learn that food was not the main attraction at the buffet bar. Some seventy-five percent of customers, I was told, were local residents rather than train-travellers and for them the attraction was the atmosphere and the beer.

There were four handpumps on a marble-topped bar above wooden panels inset with faded pictures of old steam trains. And the nectar gushing from those pumps had been good enough to make this place one of three runners-up in the Campaign for Real Ale's national Pub of the Year competition.

Not bad for a buffet bar – even one with a fine open fireplace and a decorative piano. The piano hadn't been played for some time. According to one long-standing regular, the last man to tickle the ivories had sounded "like Les Dawson on a bad night".

Yes, Les Dawson. That takes you back. One of the great deadpan comedians of his day was born just up the line in Manchester and died two years after my first visit to Stalybridge. It was so long ago, in fact, that the station was still owned by British Rail.

Mind you, in that immediate post-Thatcherite era BR was under pressure to flog off its old station buildings to an entrepreneur. Somebody from BR's Property Board told me at the time that the buffet "suggests wine bar or restaurant use".

Over fifteen thousand residents and travellers resented that suggestion enough to sign a petition against it. Maybe that was one reason why the buffet bar was still open and still much as it had been when I returned some years later. By that time I was a contributor to the *Telegraph's* Pint to Pint column. Still am, now and again. Or as least I was until the latest lockdown locked us out.

And there's the rub. As I write, more and more pubs have had to close down – not just at 10 pm but for good. Admittedly that was happening BC (Before Corona). Since the turn of the century, the UK has lost almost a quarter of its pubs.

Those permanent closing times came about for any number of reasons: everything from road-widening schemes to redevelopment projects. For the most part, however, the cause was rising rents and declining footfall. Small inns have found it increasingly difficult to compete with large supermarkets offering cut-price booze and spacious car parks.

The pandemic has simply accelerated an ongoing process. Around five percent of all remaining pubs closed in the year since the first lockdown came into force in March 2020.

In those pubs that remained open until the second national lockdown, there were strict rules to ensure some social distancing. No more swapping yarns while standing at the bar. You had to sit at a table, usually pre-booked, and wait to be served. Then you could remove your mask and have a drink – once, that is, you'd focussed your phone on the track-and-trace app.

This book was written entirely during the third lockdown. I finished the last chapter on April Fools Day, although there are a couple of lat additions towards the end of Chapter Six.

Fears for the future of our pubs may well seem to have been exaggerated by the time that you read this and, hopefully, the pandemic may seem part of the past. A particularly painful past, I might add, for those who have lost ones to its vicious grip. But just now feels like a fitting moment to reminisce about those heady pre-panademic days, for the most part, and the "inns" that Belloc all too evidently relished and cherished.

I've been lucky enough to be paid for visiting a fair few inns over the years. Not just in England and not just for national newspapers. In the 1970s I had a column called Pub Call when I was a feature writer on what was then the *Nottingham Evening Post*. And for a while in the '80s, there was Pubscrawl in the *Coventry Evening Telegraph*, where I was features editor.

Introduction

So I'll be reminiscing about hostelries in those cities and others where I've been a resident: London for one, Birmingham for another. First, though, let's set off on a tour of some of those eccentric alehouses. Some will have changed beyond recognition. Others will have closed, sometimes reopening under new management before closing again. It's difficult to keep track in such turbulent times.

Perhaps we ought to treat these reminiscences as just that – my personal memories of moments in time when many more inns could still afford to stay open.

Inns, taverns, hostelries – call them what you will – have been threaded through the cities, towns and villages of this small island for centuries. The stories around them are part of the local folklore and national distinctiveness. All that we can hope is that one day normal service is resumed in enough of them to maintain that distinctiveness, their character and indeed the characters who use them.

An all-too-typical sign outside a village pub once full of eccentricities

Closing Time

Chapter One

Landladies with Staying Power

The reason why so little had altered at the Case is Altered, one of the Warwickshire watering holes that I mentioned in the introduction, was largely down to long-serving landlady Jackie Willacy. She was there when our mini-bus of Anglo-French pub crawlers called in in the early '90s, and she's still there now. At least she was the last time I checked. You never know in these uncertain times.

It was back in the early '70s when she started working behind the bar with her grandmother, who had been the licensee for over forty summers before that. Grandma eventually bequeathed the family's free house to Jackie. And Jackie and her husband Charlie bought out her "business partner" in 1987.

Customers kept outside the Case in the plagued summer of 2020

Closing Time

Jackie sent me some photographs during the lengthy closure brought about by the virus. Among the few changes that I could make out were new leather (or leatherette) covering on the settles and the springing up of handpumps on the bar. Exit Ansell's bitter and mild straight from the barrel. Enter other draught ales including those from the Old Pie Factory brewery in nearby Warwick, where the Willacys' son Josh is head brewer.

Food?

You can bring your own sandwiches – "as long as you buy the crisps off us," Jackie insists.

The same pub ready to welcome customers back one of these days

She is one of quite a few longstanding landladies that I've met over the years running similarly unspoilt survivors. Some have been granddaughters of long-serving licensees. Others have been daughters or widows of publicans past

1 - Landladies with Staying Power

Mabel Mudge retired on October 4, 1994, her 99th birthday. For seventy-five years she had been at the Drewe Arms in the village of Drewsteignton, not far from Exeter. "Auntie Mabel", as she was known to the regulars, had run this thatched and white-washed ale-house since 1951 when her husband Ernest had died. In that time she had presided over one major change: the installation of running water and electricity.

The Drewe Arms, thatched, whitewashed and bedecked with flowers

Unfortunately, I never had the privilege of meeting Mabel. But I did spend a memorable Monday evening at this 17th century, Grade II* listed building in 1995. I'd driven there down expansive motorways followed by lanes as "narrow and high-sided a bobsleigh run", to quote from a piece that I wrote not for the *Guardian* or *Telegraph* but the *Independent*, then a broadsheet newspaper. And since you ask, no, I did not drive back. Stayed somewhere nearby, as I vaguely recall.

Closing Time

Like the regulars, I'd helped myself to Flowers IPA, served straight from the cask and handed the cash to long-standing barmaid Elaine Chudley.

Mudge and Chudley are two names with a distinctively Devonian ring about them. Elaine told me that the Egon Ronay plaque on the front of the pub had caused some confusion in the summer-time when visitors from near and far are prevalent in Devon. "They come in expecting heaven knows what delicacies," she'd confided. "All I can offer them is bread and cheese and my mum's ham sandwiches."

It seems that the inspector from Egon had welcomed a change from the fancy food served in many a pub-restaurant. Instead, he or she had evidently revelled in generous chunks of home-cured ham clamped between crusty white bread that had been smothered with butter by Elaine's mum, Dorothy Fox. She was then seventy-six and had worked for Auntie Mabel since the 1950s.

On the evening of my visit the food on offer was somewhat more exotic – a tasty casserole of chicken and black-eyed beans with mushrooms and onions. There was cinnamon and garlic in there. Cumin and coriander too. Not forgetting the rice. All had been cooked by a local resident who ran a nearby restaurant and had apparently trained with Keith Floyd.

Well, it was a Monday, and Mondays offered something new for the Drewe – a weekly "food evening". Local residents cooked at home, ferried the food to the pub and heated it up on Auntie Mabel's old Rayburn.

All money raised from this and other fund-raising events went to the Save the Drewe campaign, set up by villagers to stop the pub being sold off and either closing down or changing beyond recognition in the era PM: Post-Mudge.

Gone would be those new-fangled electric light bulbs dangling from a glossy ceiling of nicotine brown. (Smoking inside pubs was still allowed

1 - Landladies with Staying Power

in those days.) Gone too would be walls covered with photos of the village cricket team and the roaring fire that seemed in danger of melting the plastic darts' flights resting on the mantelpiece.

And was the Drewe saved?

It seems so, judging by comparatively recent pictures on-line, including food offers somewhat more varied than Dorothy's delicious ham sandwiches.

As I write, the pub is closed. It may or may not reopen. According to Steve Murray, chair of Camra's Exeter branch, it reopened after the first lockdown but closed down again in high summer. Rumours of a rift between the licensee and the owners, apparently. "Before we could investigate properly, the landlord had gone and the pub was closed," Steve revealed.

Hopefully it will reopen once more in the not too distant future. After all, this is a handsome building inside as well as out. It's rated by CAMRA's guide to Historic Pub Interiors as of "national importance".

Mabel Mudge must be turning in her grave.

* * * *

Now let's head further south into this glorious county – as far as Widecombe, famous for its fair still staged in early September. Until 2020, needless to say, when Uncle Tom Cobley and all couldn't be allowed to mingle freely at such a popular attraction.

The Rugglestone Arms, tucked away on the outer edge of the village, had also become popular – "beer still served straight from the barrel," I was assured by south Devon Camra spokesman Andrew Thomson, "and excellent food."

There was no food served when I was there back in 1992 to do a piece for *The Guardian*. A Cornish pastie from the village post office put a lining on the stomach as I followed my guide for the day down a dung-splattered lane.

The Rugglestone in more recent times

Arthur Sandford, assistant coach to the British swimming team at the 1968 Olympics, had long ago left his native Devon. But here he was making a nostalgic journey "home" after a driving us nigh-on two-hundred miles that very morning. Arthur had never lost his West Country "burrrr". Or indeed his "thirrrst" for life in general and draught Bass in particular. That's what he drank at the Town Wall Tavern in Coventry where we'd first met. And that's what he was evidently intent on now, judging by the increase in pace as we drew closer to the oasis of the Rugglestone.

I recall tossing the remains of my half-digested pastie to a sheepdog that had been following us with its tongue lolling from an all too evidently watering mouth. Then I had to put on a spurt of speed to catch up with the swimming coach as the pub's granite exterior hove into view.

1 - Landladies with Staying Power

As for the interior, that was very much the home ground of Audrey Lamb, the landlady who had lived here for all of her nigh-on sixty years. Her father Harry Lamb had doubled as licensee and village stone mason. Only one thing had changed at the Rugglestone since his day: the removal of a hoop-throwing game similar to quoits from the back of the door that led off a passageway populated entirely by locals. Beyond that door was the hallowed sanctuary of the front parlour. Passageway and parlour were also linked by a hatchway servery, behind which were barrels of Bass and cider.

The door latch seemed to crack like a pistol shot as we made our way into that inner-sanctum where a large man was pumping at the open fire with a pair of bellows while his small dog looked on.

The only other two customers were discussing Joe Louis's fight with Tommy Farr as though it had happened yesterday. They were also supping bottles of Toby light ale.

Hardly Arthur's thing, needless to say. Nor mine. We'd both called for pints of Bass. He'd slid on to a narrow wooden settle with a back so high that it almost reached the beamed ceiling. Meanwhile, I'd found a chair by a table from a farmhouse kitchen that had been covered with a brown oil cloth, pitted here and there with cigarette burns.

We'd both been eyed suspiciously when we walked in. After all we were unexpected strangers. Probably "crackles", as holidaymakers are known in these parts. But once Arthur's Devonian drawl was clocked, the boxing discussion resumed. So did the bellows pumping.

After a while Audrey came in to warm herself by the fire and lob on another log. By which time the conversation had moved on to reminiscences of the former village sexton Harry Bray and his taste for a powerfully fermented cider from a nearby farmhouse. Took a gallon with him when he helped out at harvest time, we were told, and came back for a refill before breakfast.

Closing Time

"He could drain a quart jug within an inch of the bottom with one swig," Audrey recalled. "I can see him wiping it off his whiskers."

Will we ever hear conversations like this in pubs like that again?

It seems increasingly unlikely.

In more recent years I'd lost touch with Arthur. Only when I Googled his name did I discover that he had "passed away peacefully" in May, 2020. He was eighty-four. Six years previously I'd thought about him during a visit to the Pattenmakers Arms in Duffield, Derbyshire, another pub that served Bass straight from the barrel. It was ferried from the cellar in three-pint jugs.

The Pattenmakers where Bass was served in three-pint jugs

Luckily, there were three of us sharing a table. I'd met up on Derby Station with two old friends from Nottingham. They were "only here for the beer", to quote from an advert for a mercifully long-forgotten fizzy and cloying keg product called Double Diamond. Needless to say, I was on my way to carry out a diligent piece of research – for the *Telegraph* Pint to Pint column on this occasion.

1 - Landladies with Staying Power

Yes, I enjoyed the Bass. And, yes, I enjoyed the faggots and peas served with a rich gravy and delivered from the kitchen by the same hard-working manageress, Emily Bowler, who had lugged another jug of Bass from the cellar not too long previously.

The licensee Claire Muldoon was away for a few days on a well-earned holiday. Her reward for greatly increasing trade since taking over the pub six years previously had been an all-too-typical forty-two percent rent increase from Enterprise Inns. Such impositions have been the reason for so many pubs losing their economic viability and having to close their doors.

On this occasion the company backed down in the face of a huge petition and the lobbying of the Business Secretary by the local MP and the GMB union. The Pattenmakers survived. And, hopefully, it will come through an unprecedented period of lockdowns and restrictions on social mixing.

* * * *

Time, perhaps, to head back west once more. And even further back in time. To the reign of Rene, better known as "Auntie Rene" – or Irene Jelf, to give the longstanding landlady of the Boat Inn at Ashleworth Quay in Gloucestershire her correct title. She and her sister Sybil had inherited the pub from their father and, since the death of Sibyl in 1990, Irene had run it with the help of her niece Jackie.

Generations of Jelfs had kept the Boat afloat – all too literally at times. Until the advent of better flood defences, there had been an annual battle against water penetrating the building from the nearby River Severn. (Legend had it that the family's right to ferry folk across the water had been granted by Charles II in 1651, after he had fled from the Battle of Worcester and been rowed to safety by a Jelf.)

Water levels were low, or comparatively so, when I arrived at Ashleworth Quay to do a piece for the *Guardian* column sometime in the 1990s. Only three years previously Auntie Rene had been serving beer in her gum boots while standing in a foot and a half of water. "The regulars had to collect their waders from the tithe barn up the road," she chuckled.

The Boat Inn on a day when a boat was required to get in

One of those regulars would have been Jim Kilpatrick who was enthroned on his high-backed settle soon after noon, his large hand lovingly cupped around a pint of cider. Wisps of white hair protruded from under a battered cap above a well-weathered face, and big boots were planted on a rush mat over a well-scrubbed flagstone floor. The only water that floor had come in contact with on that particular morning had come from a cleaner's bucket.

Jim was soon reminiscing about the local sport of elver-eating. The Boat had been one of several riverside pubs where regulars occasionally competed to see how many baby eels they could swallow in a timed session. Until, that is, elvers were priced out of the market. "They used to be a poor man's meal," Jim had confided. "Lovely when fried up with a bit of bacon fat. Now they sell them abroad. Last I heard they were thirty-nine quid a kilo."

Auntie Rene would have cooked them in her black-leaded range in the days when regulars used to dry out while sitting in her kitchen. The range was still there when I looked around, but there had been some comparatively recent modernisation of the bar – a discreet gas radiator here and a new wall light there.

Elsewhere on the walls were pictures with a distinctively '50s flavour. One of them showed a pneumatic blonde in tight leopard-skin trousers. Her facial expression bordered on ecstasy as she sipped a glass of Double Diamond, believe it or not.

I was far happier in real life, seeing off a ploughman's lunch worthy of the name eased down by a pint of Smiles, a Bristol brew which, like the cider, had been served straight from the barrel. Smiles slipped down my throat and smiles occasionally lit up my face as the conversation took on a philosophical turn. When does lamb become mutton? And, more importantly here on the banks of the Severn, when does an elver become an eel?

Descendants of the Jelfs still owned the pub as 2020 was coming to an end. But the Boat remained closed. That may well have changed by the time you read this. We live in hope.

* * * *

Madge Farnsworth could have been a character from *Coronation Street*. Had she come from 't'other side of 't' Pennines, that is.

Yes, we've moved a long way north, beyond Derbyshire and into Yorkshire. To the Cardigan Arms, to be precise, on the Kirkstall Road in Leeds where Madge was holding court in the public bar under a framed photo of the Hunslet rugby league team (1937-38).

It was 1993 at the time and Madge was a sprightly seventy-five. Thirty years previously she had managed to secure a small flat next door to her beloved local when the warren of terraced streets across the road had been flattened in the cause of redevelopment.

"It were seething in here at one time," she confided. "So much beer was spilt it was running out the door in little streams."

Closing Time

The Cardigan Arms lit up BC: Before Corona

Tetley's was the beer, needless to say. Still brewed in Leeds at that time and served in the traditional Yorkshire way, with a tight sprinkler to provide a thick and creamy head. Madge worked her way steadily through nine halves of it a night. Not always in the bar, mind you. Not in the "old days". Then she would have been found in the snug known locally as the "Nanny Hole" – until, that is, one of its more venerable regulars set fire to the curtains with one of her Capstan Full Strength cigarettes.

That was in 1968, apparently. One aspect of the Nanny Hole had survived by 1993, however. You could still see the words "Ladies Only" etched into the glass while standing in the corridor, serenaded by Frank Sinatra from what I termed in the *Guardian* column "a heritage jukebox". You could also see the fine curved mahogany main bar, bordered by a gleaming brass rail.

To the left were the Blue Room and the Oak Room with their huge, gilt-framed mirrors and marble fire places. And through the half-open kitchen door someone was beating batter with much vigour. Yes, Yorkshire pud was the mainstay of the menu. The size of the average wok, each one was filled with beef or lamb awash with gravy.

It was in that corridor that I'd first had the privilege of meeting another former resident of those flattened terraced streets across the road. Joyce Kennedy not only looked and sounded like a character from *Coronation Street*; she'd actually been one. Played Alma Walsh, apparently, who'd run the Flying Horse at a time when Annie Walker was still the dominant figure behind the bar at the Rover's Return.

Had a rich and resonant voice did Joyce. She'd been a night-club singer in her time. But it was her performances as Alma in "Corrie" that had apparently impressed the managing director of Tetley's in the '70s. He'd made it plain that he expected life to imitate art when she and her husband Trevor had been offered the Cardigan on a six-month trial. "That was fifteen years ago," Joyce told me.

And nearly thirty years on from that chat with a landlady from *Coronation Street* and Kirkstall Road?

Well, the website points out that this Grade II listed pub had been "restored to its former glory" by Kirkstall Brewery – one of heaven knows how many "micros" to have blossomed in the 21st century. The food offer seemed to be somewhat more upmarket than meat-filled Yorkshires. There were some Vietnamese options on the menu, if you please, and booking was recommended to guarantee a table.

But as I write, Leeds is in tier three of the Covid countering restrictions. Hopefully the Cardigan will be unbuttoned and reopened one of these days.

* * * *

It was coming to the end of what had seemed like a long day. I'd driven 175 miles and, after lengthy traffic jams on the A64, had finally made it to Scarborough's fabled festival of cricket along with over 5,000 others. Most of them were Yorkshiremen. Some of them were holidaymakers. One of them was my publisher at the time.

Graham Coster had travelled up from London the day before and stayed overnight. It was Graham who had commissioned me to write four of the Britain's Lost series for Aurum, including Britain's Lost Cricket Festivals. Which meant that I had to be at St George's Road, Harrogate, the following morning to gather memories of one of Yorkshire's many former out-grounds. Back to the car then at close of play, followed by a drive of a mere sixty miles or so.

Betty's Tea Room, something of a Harrogate institution, had long closed by the time I arrived. But I remember walking past the premises after managing to get a late-ish meal at a pub the name of which I can't recall. I also circumnavigated the vast bulk of the Crown Hotel on my way towards my somewhat more humble resting place.

Time for an early night, perhaps?

Or maybe not.

The legacy of William Hales

1 - Landladies with Staying Power

Certainly not after I'd stumbled across an intriguing-looking hostelry that didn't so much gleam as glow in the dark. Hales' Bar turned out to be lit entirely by gas mantles, just as it would have done in 1882 when the eponymous William Hales had become landlord.

Ancient barrels and stuffed birds were vaguely visible behind the bar. On the bar, meanwhile, ornate brass cigar lighters nestled between the handpumps. Smoking had been banned in pubs by then but visitors in the winter months liked to warm their hands upon them. Or so I was told once I'd decided to stay for a small *digestif*.

... and still gas-lit in the 21st century

Sometime later I emerged after discovering that licensee Amanda Wilkinson liked a party. So, it seemed, did many of her regulars.

Having fallen into conversation with a visitor from Devon, I spotted something else through the atmospheric lighting. There was a piano that looked as though it was begging to have its ivories tickled. As luck would have it, the Devonian I'd been chatting with turned out to be a cocktail-bar pianist. And it didn't take long to persuade him to regale us with a tune or two.

Considerably more than two, as it turned out. He ran through a lengthy repertoire, from "free 'n' easy" to boogie-woogie. Ensconced as they were in decorative gas-lit alcoves, the clientele responded by singing along enthusiastically and, in some cases, getting up to dance.

So much for Harrogate's reputation as a pillar of rectitude. And so much for my plans for an early night.

On a much chillier November day in the same year (2013) I returned to Hales in Harrogate to do a piece for the Telegraph column. At the bar was a man who'd just walked and was warming his hands on a cigar lighter that had flared like a Bunsen burner. I'd just asked for an Old Legover – brewed in Harrogate and "sited next to the Dizzy Blonde on this bar lined with brassy taps and priapic pumps", to quote from my piece in Pint to Pint. As I put in my order, I peered at the stuffed birds behind the barrels. Among the great auks and bustards was a scale-model of Tweety Pie. Amanda Wilkinson, it would seem, had a chirpy sense of humour as well as a liking for a party. She has run Hales Bar single-handedly since 2003. "I just helped out when it was put up for lease and ended up getting the job," she told me. She also told me that she's started in the pub trade at eighteen. That was a mere thirty-three years ago. Plenty of life left in Amanda. And, hopefully, she'll be back behind the cigar lighters, ensuring that there's plenty of life and gas-light left in Hales Bar, if and when we return to a semblance of normality.

Chapter Two

Redoubtable Landlords

On February 4, 1793, Burnham Thorpe's most famous son held a bit of a "do" in the hostelry at the heart of the Norfolk village that he was about to leave for the last time. His ship, the Agamemnon, was waiting. In the Napoleonic wars that followed he would lose his eye, his arm and, eventually, his life. But he would gain a hell of a reputation.

Quite by chance, I arrived at the Lord Nelson almost 200 years to the day after Horatio's departure party. My chauffeur on that occasion had been Pat McMahon, a strapping Irishman who ran the Coombe Abbey pub (sadly long-gone) in the heart of Coventry's former watch-making district. Pat always enjoyed socialising. The only thing he liked more than mingling with customers on their side of the bar was mingling with customers in someone else's bar.

The Lord Nelson Pub in Burnham Thorpe is now owned by the Holkham Estate and was due to reopen in the Spring of 2021, viral restrictions permitting, after a prolonged project of restoration.

He'd first found himself in the Lord Nelson thanks to an old pal called Gil Howat, a former Cumberland wrestler and police inspector who'd retired to his beloved north Norfolk coast some years previously. I would be introduced to Gil later. But first Pat introduced me to Les Winter, licensee and local historian of all things Nelsonian.

Les was a rum character in more ways than one. Indeed he produced a rum that he named after the much celebrated naval commander. It was called "Nelson's Blood" and was a fearsome concoction of Wood's hundred percent mixed with spices to give it a reddish tinge as well as a distinctive flavour. Fiery passage from throat to stomach could be eased by chasing it down with gulps of Greene King Abbot. A high-strength ale at the best of times, it was even stronger than usual by the time Les had given it his special treatment.

No, he didn't top it up with rum. Instead he defied all the normal laws of beer-keeping by "laying it down for a while to mature", as though it was a vintage wine. Every now and then Les would shuffle off in his slippers and return with a dark and brooding brew drawn straight from the barrel.

"I've never had beer like it," fresh-faced Gregory Sheppard confided to the *Guardian's* diligent Pub of the Month correspondent. A student of the viola at the Royal Academy, young Gregory told me that he occasionally travelled by train from King's Cross to King's Lynn, by bus to Hunstanton and then by foot a dozen miles or so to Burnham Thorpe. Sometimes he borrowed a bike from friends nearby for the return journey. "But if I have four pints and a 'Blood', I have to push it," he admitted.

We were chatting in a bar with a surprisingly clean whitewashed ceiling. No nicotine-yellow staining up there. Les had given up smoking nearly twenty years previously and, more recently, had decided that his customers should do the same. Bear in mind that the legal ban on smoking in public spaces, including public bars, was still thirteen years away at the time of our visit.

2 - Redoubtable Landlords

Nigh-on seventy pictures of Nelson and his ships bedecked the walls of the pub from settle-tops to ceiling. One was of The Victory sailing out of a fog of nicotine into a clear blue sky. The caption beneath read: "Victory emerging from your smoke screen. Nearly five years of gunge on the left."

And if that wasn't warning enough, a hand-written no smoking notice had been scrawled on folded cardboard and placed on each rough-hewn table.

Heaven knows what the retired colonel who'd called in early one evening would have made of this bizarre bar where you could chat with anyone from a former Cumberland wrestler to a budding viola player. Unfortunately for the colonel, he'd made the mistake of addressing Les like a lowly army private rather than a naval historian. "Is this the only room you have?" he boomed.

"How many rooms do you want?" came the curt response.

"Well, I have three ladies in the car and I want to know if it's suitable to bring them in."

"It was good enough for Admiral Lord Nelson. If it's not good enough for you, you can bugger off."

The pub is now owned by the Holkham Estate and was due to reopen in the Spring of 2021, viral restrictions permitting, after a prolonged period of restoration.

* * * *

Time, perhaps, to head north. Way up north and across the border to the Scottish capital where, somewhat confusingly, there's a pub called the Oxford Bar. Anybody with an Oxford accent, however, would have had difficulty getting served in the days of the late landlord Willie Ross. He presided over the pumps from the year after the end of the Second World War until the early 1980s.

Closing Time

Thankfully, I arrived on a Friday evening a decade or so after his departure. Englishmen, I was told, were barely tolerated during his lengthy reign. Neither was anybody seeking more than liquid sustenance. A customer who had the audacity to ask for a packet of crisps was allegedly dragged outside and asked if there was anything on the front of the building to suggest that this pub was a restaurant.

An apocryphal tale, perhaps?

Well, the Oxford Bar has always attracted story-tellers, including Ian Rankin who celebrated a comparatively recent birthday with a pint outside his favourite Edinburgh pub. He couldn't go inside during the lockdown, needless to say. And, yes, the Oxford features in his Inspector Rebus novels.

As for the poet Forbes Macgregor, he once penned an ode to Willie Ross. It was pointed out to me, somewhere on a wall in the compact front bar. Eventually, that is. When I'd first arrived, the place was packed with smartly suited figures swigging pints and arguing stridently. And that was just the women among many representatives of the legal profession.

My progress to the "side room" entailed skirting round piles of discarded black briefcases with gold fittings. Not easy when you were carrying a pint of Boddington's (made in England at the time) and a local delicacy called a "bridie" – a pie packed with mince and onions.

As the evening wore on and the lawyers headed home, the main bar started to fill with burly farmers, up from the Borders or down from the Highlands. They were draining pints of comparatively local Belhaven with gusto while discussing Scottish rugby. With an Englishman, what's more. Yes, I was not just tolerated but made welcome thanks to the wry good humour of the licensee of the time, one John Gates.

Far more welcoming than Willie would have been. But in a city blessed with many stylishly tiled and ornately decorated bars, John had kept the Oxford simply furnished, much as it always had been under Ross's rule. Pews still lined the walls of the side room where I'd seen off my bridie. And a striking picture of Rabbie Burns still hung by the doorway.

Admittedly, a television had been installed above and just to the right of the optics. Only turned on for rugby internationals, I was assured. And as I recall, Scotland were hosting one the following day at Edinburgh's Murrayfield stadium.

Thankfully, England were not the away side on that occasion. Otherwise my burly drinking companions on that memorable Friday may not have been quite so hospitable.

* * * *

While on the subject of rugby, let's make a foray across another border – into Wales where the national game is oval-balled and the desire to beat England just as fierce.

Hence the salted hams dangling from the ceiling of the Tafarn Sinc, a tavern built of corrugated iron and clinging to a hillside at the end of a disused railway in the Pembrokeshire village of Rosebush. One of those hams would traditionally be brought down and carved up whenever the Welsh had beaten their nearest neighbours – almost a guarantee in the 1970s but less common in the '90s.

"We took one down after the last international against England, even though we lost," I was told by the licensee's daughter Hafwen Llewelyn, taking a break from pumping up Hancock's HB. The ham had been up there for so long that it was tough as old rugby boots, apparently. Salty, too, which at least may have made the regulars even thirstier than usual.

Salted hams dangling from the ceiling of the well-renovated Tafarn

Hafwen's father Brian Llewelyn was a ruddy faced businessman with a packet of cigars protruding from his top pocket. The Tafarn had been somewhat run down when he'd taken it over from another of those long-serving landladies a few years previously. Peg Lewis had died in 1992 after serving behind the bar for fifty-two years.

Little had changed in that time, I was told, after driving over two hundred miles and clocking up considerable expenses from the *Guardian*. Bed and breakfast was available nearby, despite Rosebush never becoming the prosperous spa town that the owners of the

Maenclochog slate railway had gambled on when they had the pub built, or rather slotted together, in the 1870s.

Some 120 years on and beer was still being served straight from the barrel. Worthington Bitter, apparently. And on Saturday nights Peg's grandson Ian would still let rip on a powerful organ imported from the Masonic Hall in Haverfordwest. "It was so loud, the boards used to go up and down," recalled John Griffiths, a farm worker known to all as Captain. "How we didn't finish up in the cellar I'll never know."

Captain also confided that the aforesaid cellar was full of wild cats that kept fit by chasing rats. It seems that Brian Llewelyn must have had quite a job on his hands when he'd taken over the Tafarn in 1992. The renovations took six months and included painting the corrugated iron frontage maroon and cream as well as creating a garden where Rosebush Station once stood.

Inside, as I recall from my visit a quarter of a century or so ago, the boards had been nailed down and an ancient route map of the Great Western Railway hung over a wood-burning stove. Nearby, Captain was chatting in Welsh while wedged on to one of several handsome settles with a character called Jack Owen. Thankfully they switched to English for my benefit and began to reminisce about pre-war days when the Maenclochog Railway was still open.

Apart from slate, there were times when it apparently conveyed rabbits down to Clynderwen where they were transferred to the Great Western and despatched to Birmingham market. "Peg paid me sixpence a head for each one," Jack recalled.

Captain nodded sagely. "She knew a bit about meat did Peg. A butcher's daughter she was."

Heaven knows what she would have made of those tough and salty hams hanging from her ceiling. And they couldn't even be brought down when Wales won the Five Nations in March 2021 for obvious reasons.

Closing Time

* * * *

And so "across the water" we go. Not from Liverpool to Ireland but a somewhat shorter "ferry cross the Mersey" to Birkenhead.

I arrived feeling somewhat bristly, not having shaved that morning. Well, Gallagher's was billed as a barber's as well as a bar. And former Irish Guardsman Franky Gallagher was as adept with a razor as he was at keeping draught ales from nearby breweries. It was easy to see why this had been voted Camra's Merseyside Pub of the Year 2011 and 2012.

Image courtesy of https://www.hotspotmedia.co.uk/

Apart from the beer, the surroundings were impressive too – plenty of dark wood lit up by a vaulted ceiling of decorative glass and covered up in parts by pictures of ocean-going liners on the Mersey, submarines made at nearby Cammell Laird and memorabilia from Franky's Guardsman days.

To quote from one of my Pint to Pints that appeared in a hardback collection of those columns published by the *Telegraph* in 2016, "A piano regularly bursts into life under the skilled fingers of Peter the Pianist: Rachmaninov one minute, 'Roll Out the Barrel' the next. And there are regular bi-monthly poetry nights featuring the Roger McGoughs and Adrian Henris *de nos jours* in the cocktail bar upstairs."

No sooner had I savoured the first swig of Trapper's Hat, a fruity yet bitter-edged brew from somewhere in the Wirral, than I was called through for my appointment with a cut-throat razor.

A hot towel was about to be swathed over my face as a prequel to the shaving soap when I glimpsed something from the corner of my eye. On a shelf between barber's and bar was a glass cabinet for keeping pies hot.

You won't be surprised to learn that Sweeney Todd came to mind. And, no, I don't suppose that I was the first to point this out shortly before the "cut-throat" flashed around my neck. "We fill that cabinet on Saturday lunchtimes," Franky explained, as he must have done before many a shaving.

Saturdays were when discerning football fans from far and wide came for away matches at Prenton Park, the nearby ground of Tranmere Rovers. And what more would a match-bound fan want than a pie and a pint or three?

"The Coventry City supporters were great," Franky went on as the razor went up to cheeks and chops. "They ate all the pies in fifteen minutes and seemed to love the place."

No doubt there would have been quite a few supporters of the home side there as well and no doubt they would have noticed. There would have been little doubt about the prevailing chant from their end of the ground once footballing hostilities were underway. Yes, "you ate all the pies, you ate all the pies ..."

All I recall for sure is that I emerged from the barber's side of Gallagher's into the bar with a face as smooth as a baby's bottom. There I reacquainted myself with my pint of Trapper's Hat and one or two halves of other impeccably kept ales, including Liverpool Organic Brewery's Honey Blond from "across the water".

The Holly Bush in more recent times, albeit pre-lockdown

* * * *

Now we're off to meet a landlord who introduced himself to me as "a Liverpool gentleman". Charlie Bruchez's French father had once been head pâtissier at the Midland Hotel in Manchester. Yet we weren't "across the water" from Birkenhead, or in Manchester for that matter. We were in the Cheshire village of Little Leigh – at the Holly Bush Inn, to be precise.

Charlie was sporting a paisley waistcoat, dark trousers and shocking pink socks. "I'm the second longest-serving landlord of modern times here," he proclaimed, having held the licence all of six months. His predecessor, one Albert Cowap, had been there over fifty years.

2 - Redoubtable Landlords

By "there" I mean registered as the publican. His mother seemed to have run a building that had been in the same family for over two hundred years and had changed little in that time. Most of Albert's time was spent running twenty acres of nearby farmland, rising early and retiring to bed not long after 7.30 pm. His appearances in the tap room were brief but lively. He was a teetotaller who preferred chocolate to alcohol, apparently, and something of a philosopher who had the regulars hanging on his every word.

Charlie had made few changes since he'd taken over the running of this farmhouse-cum-pub in the 1990s, shortly after the Cowaps had finally departed. The most significant alteration had been the levering up of the hatch window between tap room and beer pumps. That had helped to reduce congestion in a passageway of worn tiles where four rooms converged.

As for the beer in those pumps, you could have Greenalls, Greenalls or Greenalls – Greenall Whitley, that is, a one-time Warrington-based brewery whose brews seemed to be all over the north-west and beyond at the time.

My visit to the Holly Bush was on a chilly autumnal Friday evening in the early nineties. Like many another research project for the *Guardian* column, I'd felt immensely glad to have found the place. Eventually, that is. It seemed like a long time since I'd left junction ten of the M56. Now here I was, gazing at an enormous picture of Edward VII casting his regal eye over the British fleet on the Solent on August 9, 1905.

I couldn't help surreptitiously casting an eye over the exceedingly attractive young woman sitting beneath that picture while sinking pints faster than anyone else in the bar. A tattooed potato picker called Kev slid into her seat after she'd waved goodbye and tottered to the door. Kev was soon enlightening us about this season's crop of Cheshires.

Nearby sat a former wholesale butcher called Bob with a strong Scouse accent and fingers covered with huge rings that gleamed in the firelight.

The Liverpool gent took a break from topping up pints every now and then to sling some coal on a fire that blazed beneath the dartboard. Such was the depth of the central beam in this timber-framed former farmhouse, that it's a wonder anybody could hit that board without throwing a dart under-arm.

Is the Holly Bush still a pub today?

Well, it certainly was when I checked on the website. Nearly thirty years previously a residents' petition and a subsequent objection by the local planning committee had saved it from being flogged off as a private residence for a wealthy family, thereby providing a fat profit for the brewery.

It may well continue to be a pub once lockdowns are behind us. But you never know. All I do know is that I was glad to be there at a certain time on a certain evening in another century.

* * * *

And so to an Oxford bar. No, not *the* Oxford Bar in Edinburgh. Been there, done that, as you may recall. Where we're going now is a bar, or rather a cosy Victorian pub, tucked away in North Parade, a mile or so north of Oxford city centre.

It was 1992 when I found myself in the Rose and Crown and overheard landlord Andrew Hall addressing three students who had just ordered a pint of Löwenbräu apiece. "That will be five pounds and four shillings, gentlemen," he proclaimed.

2 - Redoubtable Landlords

The Rose and Crown when payment was no longer required in shillings and pence

The "gentlemen" concerned looked as though they may not have been born when pre-decimal currency had been abolished over twenty-one years previously. Yet one of them handed over a tenner without so much as a query. And, yes, they received their change without a half-crown a threepenny bit or a ten bob note. They were evidently used to Andrew's funny little ways.

One wall was decorated with ice-hockey sticks while a bookcase in the passageway contained a guide to etiquette and modern manners. The menu extended from pickled eggs to a Greek salad, or you could buy pistachio nuts by the pint. "It's a lot different from the bars at home," I was told by one of the barmaids as she pulled me a pint of Brakspear's. Turned out that she came from Minnesota.

Despite the landlord's encouragement of good manners and civilised conversation, a swear box on top of the piano amassed £260 in twelve weeks — all in twenty-pence pieces, or double florins as Andrew would have called them.

Incidentally, he wasn't the only licensee that I came across with an affection for the "old money". One of them will feature in chapter Five. Another ran the Coventry Cross in Kenilworth, Warwickshire, where an ancient till still rang up payments in pounds shillings and pence well over twenty years after decimalisation. Snuff-taking by the regulars was not only allowed but encouraged in the front bar, and every year snuff tins a-plenty would dangle from the Christmas tree.

Many years later the Cross became a Michelin-starred restaurant. And the Rose and Crown?

On my one and only visit, Andrew and his wife Debbie were being threatened with an all-too-typical tripling of their rent by one of the big brewing conglomerates which had recently closed down the local brewery, Hall's of Oxford. That was nearly thirty years ago. As I write, the place is closed for the seemingly endless lockdown.

If and when it reopens, I somehow suspect that there will be no requests for payment in pounds, shillings and pence.

† *A few more redoubtable landlords may emerge in the chapters that follow.*

Chapter Three

Where it all Started

It was thirty years ago that I moved into The Shed. Yes, The Shed was in our back garden. Yes, it became my office at a time when I'd left a decently paid job as assistant editor and columnist at the *Coventry Evening Telegraph* and embarked on a career as a freelance on national newspapers. Yes, it was something of a financial gamble at a time when we still had three daughters, aged between eleven and seventeen, living at home. And, yes, peace and quiet was something of a rarity in the house.

No, I don't work in a shed these days. And, no, I don't just write about pubs. Back then I wrote feature articles about anything that I could get paid for, be it arts or education, social issues, travel, business or even motoring.

My early years as a freelance were in that long-ago era before emails became commonplace. One morning I picked up a phone call from someone on the features desk at the *Independent*, then a broadsheet newspaper. "Hull's near where you live," he informed me with the usual Londoner's sense of geography, before adding more hesitantly, "isn't it?"

"Well, it's about a hundred and forty miles away," I replied. "But I'm closer than you are. So if you're paying, I'll go."

Catching six trains a day, sometimes more, has been part of my working life for many years. Yet since the first lockdown in March, 2020, I'd been on precisely two trains in nine months. One took me all of twenty miles into the centre of Birmingham, the other five miles south of New Street to the suburb of Northfield where I was brought up and where I had my first pint.

Closing Time

Viral restrictions had lifted a little. Pubs had reopened for those prepared to sit at a suitable distance from anyone else. No standing at the bar, thank you very much. And you were expected to engage the track-and-trace app on your phone before taking a seat approved by the bar staff.

The *Telegraph*'s Pint to Pint column had restarted and I'd been commissioned to do one on the Great Stone Inn, the place where Mitchell's and Butler's Brew XI had first slid past my lips and rolled over my tongue.

Memories, memories.

The Great Stone Inn where I had my first pint

More than enough started flowing as I stepped down from the train and there to meet me was absolutely no-one. My parents had long since died and I'd lost touch with old mates I'd grown up with in Brum,

3 - Where it all Started

including one Roger Ewens with whom I'd seen off, or rather forced down, that first pint.

We were both sixteen at the time. Roger had started work in an office in the city centre while I was in my first year of the sixth-form. Obviously I didn't wear my school uniform as we surreptitiously slipped through the side door and into the "lounge bar". Roger, who seemed to know about these things, assured me that we'd have more chance of being served in there.

The adjoining public bar would have been cheaper, mind you. One shilling and ten old pence a pint for bitter and one and eight for mild, both served in straight glasses. Dimpled mugs were the preferred receptacle in the lounge, but the beer was "tuppence" dearer.

Two "bob" (10p) proved a something of a strain on my meagre resources, reliant as I then was on a Saturday job at Wakefield's army surplus stores that paid the princely sum of £1. Roger was compliant in getting me that job and, later, for introducing me to a nearby city-centre pub called the Windsor. Of that more later.

Here in the "the Stone" the landlord regarded us both with suspicion. "How old are you?" he growled.

"Eighteen," we chorused in manly unison.

"Just the one then," he eventually replied.

Sensing this less than hospitable response and conscious of the eyes of the regulars upon us, we took our pints back out into the yard and stood as far away as we could from the pungent and dimly-lit latrine that passed for the gents in those days.

Fifty-five years on and the outside gents was still there. Far more sweet-smelling and hygienic, mind you. Hot water and soap were available. Hand sanitiser, too, while the pandemic was still an all too present threat.

Closing Time

As for the yard, it was now an attractive terrace with a lawned and tree-lined area beyond. You could sit at a table and gaze at the castellated tower of the nearby church of St Laurence. Twelfth century, if you please, and a beautiful blend of sandstone and stained glass with an expansive graveyard beyond.

The building housing the Stone is also mediaeval in parts and was granted its first licence sometime in the sixteenth century. As for the "Great Stone" after which the pub was named, that was really a huge boulder that had slid here all the way downhill from Snowdon sometime in the Ice Age. To this day it's still enclosed by the thick walls and well-worn metal bars of what was once the village pound.

The pound next door to the Stone with a relic of the Ice Age behind the bars

If all this sounds somewhat rustic for Birmingham, it's a reminder that Northfield had once been a Worcestershire village. It wasn't incorporated into the city until 1911. By that time the two main local

3 - Where it all Started

employers, Cadbury's and "the Austin", were up and running. Most of our neighbours worked at one or the other.

My Dad had been an accountant, but he couldn't work anywhere for the first eight or nine years of my life. He'd contracted TB soon after my birth. And at that time it was considered incurable. Mercifully, streptomycin came to his rescue, eventually. We'd have a pint or two together at the Stone later in the '60s, when I returned from university, or the early '70s when I came back from London.

Sometimes we'd bump into Uncle Arthur, or Uncle "'alf-a" as I called him. His favourite tipple was "mixed": mild and bitter together in the same glass – a half-pint glass in his case. He'd stand at the bar seeing off one half after another at regular intervals while reminiscing about life in the navy during the war. I never did feel bold enough to interrupt and enquire why he never drank pints.

In those days the big breweries were not only spoiling traditional draught beer by pumping it full of gas; they also seemed bent on ruining many traditional hostelries by turning them into "theme pubs". As the late Basil Boothroyd once put it, your local could at any time be "misguidedly got up as the inside of a galleon, a Western saloon or, for all I know, St George's Chapel, Windsor, or a Jumbo Jet".

In the circumstances we were comparatively lucky at the Stone. There was some recognition by the re-designers that this was an ancient inn. But instead of picking out and emphasising original features, they transformed the lounge into a mediaeval pastiche made up of mock beams and brasses.

And today?

The place is infinitely better, inside as well as out. So is the beer. Impeccably kept Goff's Lancer had been brewed somewhere in the Cotswolds. With American hops, what's more. It had a citrusy edge that sharpened the appetite for a sausage sandwich from a menu that was somewhat reduced by the viral restrictions that were prevalent at the time.

My assigned table was in what was the public bar "in my day". It's now, somewhat confusingly, labelled the "Lounge". Dark wood panelling runs around the room, covered here and there by framed newspaper cuttings about the pub. One summed it up as the place "where beer is sold by the stone and pound".

Sitting under a framed page was an old friend from school whom I'd last met clipping tickets on one of my many train journeys. Since retirement from the railways he'd evidently found a haven among the weathered regulars in what was still his local.

One of those regulars had been born and brought up in Carmarthen. Suitably socially distanced on different tables, we ended up having a conversation about Welsh slate quarries. Appropriately enough, perhaps, while sitting in a pub with a little chunk of Snowdonia parked in the pound next door.

* * * *

As it happened, I knew a bit about slate quarries, having written *Britain's Lost Mines* for Aurum and *Small Island by Little Train* for the AA. Over five days I travelled on five narrow-gauge railways in Wales. Some had once conveyed slate from the quarries to the port.

Once again I'd found myself back in Blaenau Ffestiniog where, a few years previously, I'd interviewed a remarkable former blacksmith who'd worked in one of those underground hell-holes since he'd been a teenager. Went by the name of Tom Roughead and turned out to be a mine of information.

Later I checked into a B&B run by a hospitable couple from Essex. Feeling as though I'd somehow wandered into an episode of Gavin and Stacey, I then wandered out on to the high street in search of refreshment and – eventually – nourishment.

3 - Where it all Started

Side by side were a pub and a curry house. Just the job. Can't remember the name of the pub now, but it may have been the Meirion Vaults, otherwise known as the Y Meirion.

What I do remember is that everybody inside was speaking Welsh. But when I tentatively asked for a pint of bitter in English, I was served, with perfect civility, a very acceptable pint of Shepherd Neame Spitfire that had come all the way from Faversham in Kent.

I took it to a table in the corner and started going through my notes or transcribing quotes from my voice-recorder. Every now and then I'd pop out to see if there was anyone in the curry house. Nobody was.

By now I was feeling a little peckish but didn't fancy dining alone in an empty restaurant. Meanwhile, the landlady and her friends had been having a high old time, jabbering away in their first language and occasionally bursting into hysterical laughter.

Eventually one of them returned from the chip shop over the road and they were soon tucking in. The aroma was tantalising. There was nothing for it but to sidle over and blurt it out. "Can I do that?" I asked the landlady. "

"'Course you can, darling," she beamed, switching effortlessly into her second language between mouthfuls.

Battered haddock went down a treat with the Shepherd Neame and, having finished writing up my notes, I spent the last three-quarters of an hour chatting amicably to the local plumber who switched to English for my benefit.

* * * *

Now where were we? Oh, yes, in Northfield, Birmingham, where I grew up. Time, perhaps, to visit another local that I recall from my youth and young manhood.

Closing Time

You can walk to the Black Horse from the Stone. Down the road, round the corner and up . . . well, Great Stone Road. You emerge on to the busy A38 Bristol Road and there it is on the other side, difficult to miss.

Perhaps it should have been called the Black and White Horse when it was opened in December, 1929. An imposing spread of "Brewer's Tudor" for sure, it has a Grade II* listing and was designed by the architect Francis Goldsbrough on behalf of Davenport's Brewery as a replacement for a much smaller pub.

The Black Horse: a classic example of mock-Tudor pub architecture

According to the brochure of Northfield Heritage Trails, it was seen as a "reformed" pub, designed to attract a wider market than "working men". Mind you, there were more than enough working men in the public bar when I was growing up, most of them Irish and employed on nearby building sites.

There was also a Gents Only, for a while at least, and an "outdoor" – a built-in off-licence, in other words, and a useful source of extra income for those of us who weren't yet gents. The reward of threepence back on every bottle had us rifling through litter bins along the Bristol Road.

The Black Horse was also an extra source of income for my Dad. Having finally recovered from TB, he worked in "town" during the week and at the pub up the road on Saturday mornings, "doing the books" for the licensee Ray Barber.

"Uncle Ray", as I called him, occasionally invited us into the pub's palatial living quarters. On the way we passed through an upstairs function room with a hugely impressive arched and half-timbered ceiling.

Hopefully it's still there. The outside bowling-green certainly was when I last called in. That was comparatively recently while doing a job for the *Guardian* and taking a nostalgic stroll through Northfield.

The Black Horse had been Wetherspooned. There were plenty of handpumps along the lengthy bar. Not one of them dispensed Davenport's, however. Hardly surprising. The brewery had been acquired by Greenall Whitley in 1986 and closed down three years later.

Mind you, the name of Davenport's and many another venerable brewery may well have re-emerged at one of the micro-breweries that have blossomed in the UK since very welcome changes in the British beer scene began in the late eighties and continued through the first twenty years of the new century. BC, that is: Before Corona.

When I was growing up, "Davvies" was well known for supplying "beer at home". It was advertised on the telly and bottles were delivered door to door from sizeable, crate-packed vans that were open to the elements. As kids we would sometimes sidle round the back of one of those vans and climb on just before the driver started the ignition. We'd travel about two hundred yards up the road before he stopped for the next delivery. Then we'd jump down and run away.

Closing Time

Years later I discovered that Davenport's brewed the best draught bitter in Brum. Not too difficult in the era long before micro-breweries. Ansell's, then based near the Villa ground in Aston, was better known for its mild. It would become part of Allied Breweries, one of the "Big Six" brewing conglomerates, and eventually move to Burton-on-Trent after ongoing industrial unrest for much of the '70s.

As for M&B, they had been part of the Bass empire since the '60s. But until the early noughties they still brewed at Cape Hill, just over the Black Country border in Smethwick. At their peak they supplied some seven thousand pubs, including the Windsor that I mentioned earlier.

* * * *

It was to the Windsor that we repaired after those Saturdays working at the Wakefield army stores. Later we would head for dance-halls and discos "on the pick-up". But first a pint of Brew or two. Or, more often, just the one and, perhaps, a half. Had to watch the money and didn't want to sound too slurred in those studiously rehearsed disco chat-up lines.

We were still under eighteen, Roger Ewens and me. So was Tony Stokes, another good mate from those days, who worked at Wakefield's full-time and had an alluring girlfriend called Val. Very alluring when, after a couple of drinks, she'd kiss you goodbye in the narrow passageway at the back of the Windsor. It was known as Needless Alley. Still is.

The pub fronted on to Cannon Street and the front bar, known as the "public", was very much a basic boozer. Like the public bar at the Black Horse, it was full of Irish workmen from the many building sites nearby. Very lively they tended to be on Saturday evenings, shortly after being paid. Fun and laughter resounded, interrupted by occasional songs.

3 - Where it all Started

There were also occasional punch-ups and they sometimes broke out in the gents, down steep steps at the rear end of the bar. You had to pick your moment to relieve the bladder. It also felt quite a relief to be back in the lounge. Yes, there was a patterned carpet in there. And, yes, the beer was tuppence more and served in dimpled mugs.

The older clientele tended to sport trilbies, somewhat battered in many cases. They'd sit in seats that they regarded as reserved for them and converse at volume. Any attractive young woman who sauntered past on her own would stir loud comments that would be considered outrageously sexist by today's standards.

There was still a Windsor fronting on to Cannon Street last time I looked. Very different inside and more upmarket, I'm sure. But nobody can go inside at the moment. All we can do is reminisce about the way things were.

* * * *

As the '60s wore on and the '70s dawned, two factors combined to destroy much of Birmingham's rich heritage of ornate Victorian and Edwardian gin palaces. One was a tendency that I mentioned earlier for breweries to employ design consultants to "tart up" pubs by replacing the genuine with the phoney.

Victorian interiors became havens of "Victoriana", assembled in some workshop or factory the previous month.

And the other factor?

Rampant redevelopment was being allowed to ride roughshod over architectural history. "Forward" was the civic motto and the planning department seemed determined not to look back. A new ring road encircled the city centre like a vice. Pedestrians were expected to use subways. Flyovers and underpasses gave the motorcar priority. Anything that stood in their way would be bulldozed.

Attitudes had changed by the end of the '80s when councillors and planners finally realised that they would have to make the centre more appealing in order to attract visitors in the post-industrial era. But many fine buildings had already been flattened during what might be termed the "Brumbarian" era, including pubs with fine interiors and exteriors.

Some survived against the odds. Incredible odds in the case of the Barton's Arms which opened at the dawn of the Edwardian era in 1901, its exterior modelled on the nearby Jacobean Aston Hall and its interior one of the finest and most flamboyant in the country.

Carved mahogany abounded. So did Minton tiles. Some were simply arranged in decorative patterns, others in pictorial scenes. Somewhere beneath a sweeping staircase of elaborate wrought-iron, illuminated by the vibrant light spilling from a magnificent stained-glass window, was a huntsman astride his stallion in full red-coated gear. And, no, hunting was not a common pastime in inner-city Birmingham, even in 1901.

The lengthy, semi-circular bar was lined with yet more tiles and topped by snob screens. Handy, one imagines, for the music-hall stars seeking some privacy after coming offstage at the Aston Hippodrome, just across the way.

Charlie Chaplin had called in when he was on tour. Marie Lloyd, Sid Field and Enrico Caruso visited too. Somewhat more recently, Laurel and Hardy reclined at the Barton's between shows on their last tour of the UK in 1954.

The Aston "Hip" closed in 1960. Like many another theatre or cinema, it reopened as a bingo hall and closed for good in 1980. Eventually it became a centre for black and Asian arts. Sadly, that closed in 2016.

Yet the Barton's kept making comebacks, despite being bordered by a busy, six-lane highway with a rundown estate of high-rise flats on the far side, and despite being looted during the riots of 2011.

3 - Where it all Started

I'd first written about it for the *Independent* ten years previously – not for a pub column but for the Architecture section. At the time the pub was briefly locked, barred and gathering dust. Only ten years before that Mitchell's and Butler's had invested £120,000 in an extensive renovation of this priceless listed building.

Shellfish meals were on offer downstairs. Buffets abounded upstairs to attract the business market. Until, that is, the "Palace of Varieties" function room was closed in 1990 by the local fire department. The fire door was considered too close to the main door.

Exit the business market. Enter the threat of closure or an eventual reopening after extensive changes. At the time I'd speculated that it might go the way of another pub designed by James and Lister Lea – the White Swan in Bradford Street where superb Victorian tiling had been "replaced with junk 'antiques' and dusty old books to give it a 'historic theme'".

Thankfully I was wrong. The Barton's eventually reopened, restored in all its Victorian-Edwardian finery, serving Oakham Ales and Thai food.

A green curry and a pint of Citra?

Just the job in the '90s and noughties if and when I called in en-route to nearby Villa Park.

I haven't been to the Barton's for far too long. Hopefully, it will reopen to the public post-lockdown. If so, I plan to revisit. And you never know: I might even take a nostalgic trip back to the Holte End – if, by any chance, I could get hold of a ticket.

* * * *

Winson Green is another rundown part of Birmingham, best known for its formidable prison. But nigh-on thirty years ago I was lucky enough to find myself in a much more congenial and welcoming building.

Closing Time

The Bellefield was one of those listed gems that had survived against the odds. It had been set up by one Samuel White who had invested some of the "brass" from his brew-house into a nearby tap-house of colourful stained glass and exotic tilework.

The ceiling was impressive, too – "deep green and raw liver threaded with intricate patterns of gold leaf", as I described it in the *Guardian* column.

The terraced streets that had once surrounded this Edwardian gem had been bulldozed and replaced by a modern estate. As for Sam's brew-house, that had closed sometime in the 1950s.

The Bellefield would have gone the same way two decades later were it not for the intervention of the Victorian Society. It managed to secure a listing for the building.

Enter enterprising West Indian businessman Don Henry. He'd bought the pub a few years before my visit and had carried out a sensitive revamp. His family had moved from Jamaica to Birmingham when he was fifteen. And once he was old enough to start drinking, he'd developed a taste for English ale.

Knew how to keep it as well, judging by the impeccable pint of Everard's Tiger that I was presented with. Don apparently staged three beer festivals where entertainment varied from steel bands to Morris dancers.

He had plans, he told me, to reconnect the electric bell-pushes that once summoned waiters to a splendid back smoke-room. In there the Minton tiling was olive and sea-green with Art Nouveau decorations in forget-me-not blue and tan.

Screwed to a double bench bordered by high wooden partitions were brass plaques dedicated to Joe and Winn Hiscocks. Joe had recently died but Winn would be in for her daily Guinness shortly. Or so I was assured.

3 - Where it all Started

An hour later there was still no sign of her. Don duly rang her. No answer. So he went round to her house, only to discover that she'd fallen asleep, distinctly underwhelmed at the prospect of talking to the *Guardian*.

"Ah well," as I concluded the column, "Just another no-Winn situation."

And there may well be no Bellefield now. Last time I looked on-line, there was a sad picture, taken in 2013, of an empty building with those beautiful windows boarded up.

* * * *

Can't leave the city where I grew up before mentioning the pub where, by chance, I had my last pint with a good friend shortly before all pubs were closed for the first national lockdown in March, 2020.

The Old Contemptibles in Edmund Street was the venue and Ernest Taylor was the friend. Like Don Henry (see above) Ernest had arrived on these shores from Jamaica in his mid-teens and gone on to make a life for himself and his family, first as a journalist and then as an academic.

There were, needless to say, more important consequences of the lockdown than the closure of pubs – the closure of schools being one. Nonetheless, there was a sense of impending unease about being cut off from draught beer and convivial company in the very near future.

Only a month or so previously I'd been here with my wife, Jackie, to meet up with her oldest friend and her husband. We were having what you might call an aperitif before adjourning for lunch at the nearby Hotel du Vin. At that time the Corona virus was wreaking havoc on distant shores. It didn't seem like an imminent threat to our health and way of life. Or indeed to our lives.

The name of the pub and the decor around us – sepia-tinged images of soldiers from the British Expeditionary Force – was a reminder that previous generations had endured more than enough deaths.

As I wrote in the *Telegraph*'s Pint to Pint column soon after that Sunday lunchtime, "Brummie survivors of the regiment that 'put the kibosh on the Kaiser' would have pulled into nearby Snow Hill Station on returning from what was (wrongly) described as 'the war to end all wars'."

In those days the Old Contemptibles was known as the Albion Hotel, which may not have gone down well with the Villa supporters among them. Nonetheless, they continued to meet up at the pub that wasn't named after them until 1953.

Even in the '50s, veterans from a more recent world war would have been confronted by a four-ale bar (two local ales: one mild, the other bitter) and not much more to eat than a pickled egg or a corned beef sandwich.

Now there were eight handpumps ranged along the bar, offering beers from Cornwall to Cumbria. What's more, there were twenty options on the gin menu alone. As for the food menu, you could order anything from roast shallot and Armagnac tarte tatin to wild boar and chorizo pie.

On reflection it's not only two world wars that belonged to a different, very distant era. So, it seemed, did the so-called "swinging sixties" when I forced down my first pint in the back yard of the Great Stone Inn, Northfield.

Chapter Four

To London via Lancaster

The Mile End Road was busy (no change there). It was also filthy. Apart from the fumes emanating from endless lines of passing traffic, the pavement was piled with rubbish that hadn't been collected for some time. Well, the dustmen were on strike at the time.

It was October 1970 and they were demanding to be paid twenty quid a week. That would have been more than I was going to earn in my first job in journalism. On a magazine in Soho, since you ask. And, no, it wasn't that kind of magazine, in case you're wondering.

You might also be wondering why I was in Stepney, the heart of the East End. Well, that's where my friend Pat Freestone had a flat for which he paid the princely sum of sixteen "bob" (shillings) a week – the equivalent of eighty pence in the decimalised "new money" that would be with us in a few months.

When we'd left university a few months previously, he'd assured me that I could "doss down" any time that I was "in town". Hence the sleeping bag on my shoulder as I picked my way through the litter while keeping an eye out for fat rats.

At one point I glanced up to see the Blind Beggar, a pub of some notoriety at the time. It was there that Ronnie Kray had shot Charlie Richardson's henchman George Cornell four years previously. There'd been something of an altercation between the Kray twins and the Richardsons at the Astor Club "up west" in Berkeley Square.

The Beggar has moved considerably upmarket in more recent times but, back then, it was the "tap" for Mann's Albion Brewery. Not that I had any intention of calling in to sample a brown ale anytime soon.

Pat's top-floor flat was right next door to Charrington's Anchor Brewery, and tap for that one was directly across the road. It was known as the Pearly Queen during my brief stay on the Mile End Road and had been "tarted up" into a phoney Cockney theme pub. There was a barrel organ in there somewhere and you could order jellied eels with your pint of Charrington's bitter.

Luvvly jubbly?

No.

I can't pretend that I was a connoisseur of real ale at the time, but the beer seemed sweetish and slightly gassy. And as for the eels, that local delicacy was evidently beyond the taste-buds of an incomer. I much preferred the bags of cockles and whelks delivered to some London pubs towards closing time by men with baskets, giving the impression that they'd come straight from Billingsgate market.

The Charrington's brewery tap had reverted to its original name as the Hayfield not too long after I'd left. Or so Pat assured me when we'd met up at Stepney Green tube station several decades later. By then I was researching a book on Britain's Lost Breweries and Beers and, as usual, Pat was a mine of information. Not only on London breweries but on the whole area in and around the Mile End Road where he'd once flogged fish from his old man's barrow on Saturday mornings.

Since then he'd become a respected educationalist and had recently retired from his job as principal of the Mary Ward Centre in WC1. He and his wife Carol, another old friend from university days, lived close to Greenwich Park – a setting somewhat more scenic than Stepney.

Charrington's Anchor Brewery had closed in 1975. It was now a retail park. And the former brewery tap where many workers had topped up their four free pints with a fair drop more?

That had become the Hayfield Masala with a sign on the window proclaiming "No alcohol allowed on these premises."

4 - To London via Lancaster

* * * *

A brief diversion at this point to the town a long way north of here where I'd met Pat and Carol back in the late sixties. Lancaster was then regarded as home to one of the "new" universities.

The campus was set in green fields a mile or two beyond the southern edge of the city, as if to keep the born-and-bred Lancastrians at bay. The "summer of love" it may have been when I arrived but, with a few exceptions, the local youths showed little love towards male students. We were regarded as "privileged pricks" who swaggered or sloped around town with flares flapping and hair flopping on to shoulders.

Some of the locals had haircuts that seemed to have changed little since the days of teddy boys from the previous decade. You could sense the tension and feel the imminent threat in some city-centre hostelries whenever you stepped over the threshold and ordered a pint.

One notable exception was the Shakespeare in St Leonard's Gate. Students and lecturers were made welcome by an unusually learned licensee. Conversations about obscure intellectual topics were commonplace and there were sometimes poetry readings in the function room upstairs.

But the Lancaster pub that made the biggest impression on me was the first that I stepped into on the first lunchtime of my first day in town. I'd caught the train from Birmingham New Street that morning and dumped my solitary suitcase at the "digs" where the university had based me in the suburb of Scotforth.

The landlady, Mrs Sykes, had introduced me to the other four "freshers" in residence and three of them had accompanied me on a short stroll down the road to the Boot and Shoe.

Feeling somewhat peckish, one or two of us ordered the local delicacy: meat and potato pie. None of us had savoured anything quite like it before. Pub pies in my native Birmingham had been steak and kidney, the contents of which I shudder to remember in any detail.

We saw off the "m and p" not with M&B, but with Mitchell's bitter – Mitchell's of Lancaster, that is, one of two distinctive local breweries at the time. It had more of a bitter edge to it than Mitchell's and Butler's Brew XI.

I grew to like it. I also quite liked the Boot and Shoe. For one thing the bitter was infinitely better in there than in the college bars on campus where the main offer Younger's Tartan. (Scottish keg beers made me realise why the Scots tended to order a "wee half" of whisky to see them off with.)

For another thing, the Boot briefly harboured a flirtatious and buxom barmaid who, come to think about it now, was probably old enough to have been my mother. She served in the comparatively intimate front bar where the only local to threaten me was old enough to have been my grandad. And that was only because I had mistakenly picked up his pint rather than my own and taken a sip.

As I recall, there was a bigger back lounge that sometimes staged midweek entertainment – piano-led singalongs, for the most part. Not quite what we students wanted in the era of progressive rock. Still, we saw plenty of top bands on-campus and at least once on the end of nearby Morecambe Pier.

The Boot and Shoe had changed somewhat when I checked the website during lockdown. Included were not only "pub classics" but "wood-fired pizzas" and vegetarian options such as buttered squash falafel and walnut roast. "With gravy."

Meat and potato pie was nowhere to be seen.

* * * *

Now let's get back to the jellied eels. Or perhaps not, if you don't mind. My stay opposite the Pearly Queen on the Mile End Road didn't last long. After a few weeks "crashing out" at Pat's flat, I moved to another cheap residence with another good mate from university days.

John Reed and I briefly shared a first-floor hovel in the Elephant and Castle. The toilet door was off its hinges and you could hear mice scuttling about under the bath in the kitchen.

We lived largely on takeaways, which took away rather too much of our meagre incomes. And, yes, we sometimes spent evenings in nearby pubs trying to make pints last a long time. That was because (a) London prices put a further strain on our pockets and (b) the beer was not exactly more-ish. It was becoming all too evident why so many locals called for a "light and bitter", topping up a half of draught (or, more often, keg) with a bottle of light ale.

Mind you, just down the road and into Kennington was a pub called the Old Red Lion that seemed comparatively posh. Charrington's was served from handpumps and the building was inter-war mock Tudor. It has since been Grade II listed.

Just across the road was a tube station on the Northern Line. Within a few stops I could be at Tottenham Court Road, just around the corner from my workplace in Soho Square. On Thursdays, otherwise known as "pay day", I would usually have a shilling (five pence) left, which got me as far as Charing Cross. I'd walk the rest of the way, looking forward to picking up the slim brown envelope that quite easily accommodated my weekly wage.

Lunchtime drinking was very much part of journalism in those days. The editor would arrive at the office shortly after 10 am and work for an hour and a half (sometimes three-quarters) before adjourning to his club in nearby Greek Street. He'd pop back every now and then before heading off once more and returning, somewhat flushed, an hour or three later.

Pubs were expected to close in early afternoon and not reopen until early evening. Hence the market for drinking clubs in dissolute places such as Soho. For those who could afford it, that was. Those of us at the bottom end of the magazine's pecking order went out for liquid lunches only on pay day or if someone else was paying.

I do, however, vaguely remember being in two pubs with literary connections at either end of Greek Street. One was the Coach and Horses, which would become better known as one of many haunts of the writer Jeffrey Bernard and the home of long-time licensee Norman Balon.

Bernard immortalised Balon as "the rudest landlord in Britain" in his Low Life column in *The Spectator*, and was immortalised himself by Keith Waterhouse's play *Jeffrey Bernard is Unwell*. Those were the words that appeared instead of the column when Bernard was too hungover to string any words of his own together.

It was many years after my first job in Soho that I used to browse through *The Spectator* in WH Smith's in order to read Low Life on those occasions when the columnist wasn't "unwell". All I remember about my brief first lunchtime in the Coach and Horses is that another famous magazine, *Private Eye*, was hosting one of its soirées upstairs. In return for lunch, Fleet Street hacks were expected to spill the beans on hapless colleagues for the Street of Shame column.

I don't remember very much about my first time in the Pillars of Hercules at the other end of Greek Street. Well, it was on my stag night. Such was the raucous din that I could never have eavesdropped on a conversation between Martin Amis and Ian McEwan. This was the venue where those two budding authors met up.

Or so I learnt later in life. Eventually I would read every novel that either of them had written. But back then I wouldn't have recognised them. Why should I? Amis's first book was still two years away and McEwan's five years after that.

All I did know was that a new chapter in my life was about to begin.

4 - To London via Lancaster

* * * *

After our wedding, Jackie and I moved into our ground-floor flat in Earlsfield. It was two stops out of Waterloo and not far from Wandsworth which was then the home of Young's, one of only two independent breweries in London at the time.

They were still delivering barrels on horse-drawn barrows – a novel sight on the busy streets of south-west London. Particularly so when I was taking my first driving test and two tons of chained-together horseflesh suddenly pulled out in front of me with no warning. An unscheduled emergency stop was required.

Somehow I hit the brake but not the clutch, thereby stalling the engine on a busy street that was soon honking with horns. The examiner was not best pleased. Nor was I on being told that I'd failed and thereby had to shell out for yet more expensive lessons at the Earlsfield School of Motoring.

Not that I held it against Young's for too long. How could I when their draught bitters were such a contrast with Watney's Red Barrel, Double Diamond or Courage Best topped up with a light ale?

Young's "ordinary" was anything but ordinary. It was just what the locals called for if they weren't ordering the Special, a heftier 4.5 percent alcohol by volume.

I'd like to say that I enjoyed supping both in the pubs close to our first flat. But Earlsfield was far more downmarket in those days than it is today and some of the patrons of those pubs looked as though they'd recently returned from being guests of Her Majesty at nearby HM Prison Wandsworth.

Young's stopped brewing in Wandsworth in 2006, having merged with Charles Wells of Bedford. That's where the brand is brewed today. Last time I asked for a pint of "ordinary" in a Bloomsbury boozer I was charged a fiver – about a third of my take-home pay back in the distant days of my first job in journalism.

And I wasn't paid much more when I went from the magazine to work, briefly, on the *North London Weekly Herald* in 1972. Jackie and I moved "norf" of the river to Highbury which, like Earlsfield, has become considerably more upmarket in the intervening decades. The house near Clissold Park wherein we rented a top-floor flat from a genial taxi driver known as "Arfur" is now in single ownership. Worth well into seven figures last time I looked.

As for the nearby former home of Arsenal FC, that had been converted into stylish apartments. It seemed a very long time since I was either standing on the South Bank or sitting in the press box.

One place where I would never sit or stand on match days in the dire days of football hooliganism was the nearby Bank of Friendship. Rarely had a pub seemed so misnamed, particularly when Spurs were the visitors.

Like its surroundings, the Bank had evidently become posher in the intervening decades.

* * * *

Now let's fast-forward from the '70s to the twenty-first century. One day in the, hopefully, not too distant future I plan to be on the first off-peak train to London – maybe to meet up with old friends and maybe to research another piece for the *Telegraph*'s Pint to Pint column. Maybe both. Assuming, that is, that the column resumes post-lockdown.

Whatever happens, I sincerely hope that the Doric Arch reopens come the hour, come the day. Tucked away on a sidewalk in front of Euston Station, I stroll past it on my way into "town" and look forward to calling in on my way out. It's a source of Pride. Fuller's London Pride, needless to say.

4 - To London via Lancaster

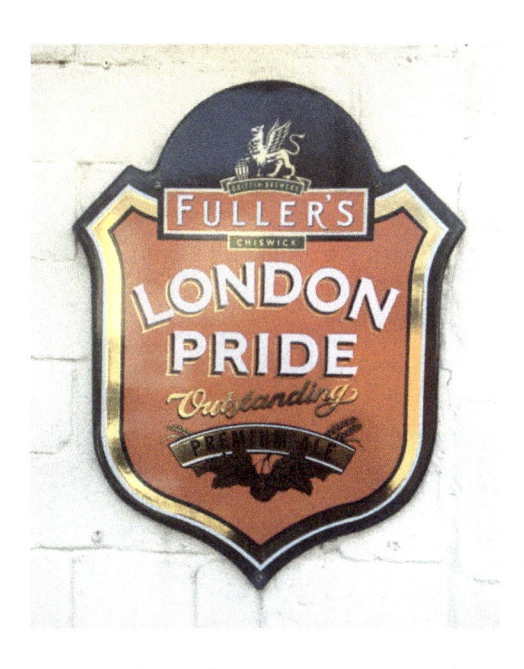

London Pride now Japanese owned

Despite its somewhat soulless setting, the Arch exceeds expectations once you've climbed the stairs to the first floor. The long bar manages to combine expansiveness with intimacy. High steps to high-backed settles at one end of the long and highly polished floorboards; close-together tables at the far end with little alcoves here and there.

Admittedly the endless news on a big screen can be mildly irritating. So can the smaller screen showing train times, especially when I glanced up and realised that I'd just missed another one. By that time I've usually been in a convivial conversation with two London-based old friends and old hacks (sorry, excellent journalists) whom I first met when we worked on the *Coventry Evening Telegraph* back in the '80s.

As for the London Pride, it's one of half a dozen handpumped beers on offer and, my goodness, it takes some beating. Hopefully it will stay like that. Along with Young's, Fuller, Smith and Turner was the other independent, family-owned brewery in London when I lived there back on the bad old days of widespread "keggery". More recently, the creation of micro-breweries had ensured a splendid spread of draught beers all over the country, including the capital.

Nonetheless, it was something of a shock to read in early 2019 that Fuller's had sold out for two hundred and fifty million to a Japanese company called Asahi, producers of a somewhat bland lager.

Roger Protz, long-time editor of the *Good Beer Guide*, proclaimed himself to be "dumbfounded". In *The Times*, meanwhile, Dominic Walsh compared the sell-out to ravens leaving the Tower of London. I found myself fondly recalling a comparatively recent visit to the brewery tap to do a piece for Pint to Pint.

The Mawson Arms finally came into view after a stroll through the streets of Chiswick, past chic boutiques, bijou houses and exclusive restaurants, followed by a trudge through a surprisingly lengthy underpass.

The reason why it was so long became evident when I eventually emerged to see six lanes of the A4. "We probably have more people going past this place than any pub in the world," mused deputy manager Simon Griffiths, gazing beyond the narrow strip of Mawson Lane towards the passing traffic beyond.

It seemed slightly surreal to see a pub sign nearby displaying rustic scenery with a huntsman trotting across it. Well, there were two pubs on this site at one time and one was called the Fox and Hounds. The F and H had long been incorporated into the Mawson, which helped to explain why the polished floor of dark and gleaming boards seemed to stretch into the middle distance.

The pub and the lane beyond were named after Thomas Mawson who was brewing on this site some time before Messrs Fuller, Smith and Turner came together in 1845. Historical pictures and ancient adverts bedecked the white walls at the far end, as I discovered after savouring a fine pint of Pride. Apart from being deputy manager, Simon had introduced himself as the "fella in the cellar". He was well aware

4 - To London via Lancaster

that the draught beers had to be in peak condition as a brewery executive could call in at any time. Or indeed a party of brewery tourists.

Traffic noise assailed the ears as soon as I left the welcome haven of the grade II* Mawson Arms. But it soon receded as I strolled down a side street past the long-time headquarters of Fuller's. Little did I know that this venerable source of Pride would soon become the UK headquarters of Asahi. Beyond was a stunning stretch of the Thames, a haven of peace and quiet as it lapped around Oliver's Island, a nine-acre clump of trees that has given its name to another fine Fuller's bitter that tasted a lot better than river water.

* * * *

Some way east of Chiswick I found myself overlooking the same river as it flowed past The Grapes in Limehouse.

The Grapes with a narrow frontage on Narrow Street and an expansive view of the Thames to the rear

As I reflected in the *Telegraph* column, "to the rear is a small balcony offering the blissful prospect of sitting with a pint on a sunny lunchtime, overlooking the Thames at high tide as it surges round the ankles of an Antony Gormley statue and slaps powerfully against the weathered London brick".

And now, to quote a slightly more eminent writer, this is how Charles Dickens described The Grapes in *Our Mutual Friend*:

"A tavern of dropsical appearance . . . long settled down into a state of hale infirmity. It had outlasted many a sprucer public house; indeed the whole house impended over the water but seemed to have got into a condition of a faint-hearted diver who has paused so long on the brink that he will never go in at all."

A century and a half since those words were quilled The Grapes was not only on dry land but looked surprisingly chipper. A few quid had evidently been spent on it. Once part of London's rundown docklands, it was now surrounded by warrens of expensive-looking apartments.

Nowhere near as expensive, one imagines, as the row of handsome Georgian survivors of the Blitz in which The Grapes still stood. Next door to the pub here on Narrow Street lived David, sorry Lord Owen, former Foreign Secretary and co-founder of the Social Democratic Party.

And the house beyond that was the home of Sir Ian McKellan, distinguished thespian and co-owner of The Grapes.

I've written all of the above in the past tense because that was the case when I was there only a few years ago. Judging by the website, it doesn't look as though much has changed. Apart from the lengthy lockdown closure, that is. The promise to reopen as soon as possible seems more than likely for an inn that has been something of a survivor over many centuries.

4 - To London via Lancaster

The current building dates from 1720, but there has been a tavern on this site since 1583. Which means that it would have been open for business the following year when Sir Walter Raleigh embarked on his epic journey to the New World from a nearby pebbly beach, exposed at low tide on the Thames. Whether he and his crew called in for a flagon of two of ale before setting sail is not recorded, as far as I know.

Somehow I doubt that the crew would have been treated to one of the house specialities on my visit: chips with battered haddock from Billingsgate Market. I also doubt that any ale from those distant days would have been as good as the Black Sheep bitter.

Mind you, I'm told on good authority that the Black Sheep had more recently been replaced as a regular among many ever-changing guest beers by Timothy Taylor's Landlord.

There always seems to be a market for Yorkshire ales here in the capital city. And at least one brewery from "oop north" has its own London pubs to supply them.

Handsome pubs, too. They include the Princess Louise in Holborn, where even the gents are listed as being of architectural interest, and the Old Cheshire Cheese, a fabled Fleet Street haven since not too long after the Great Fire of London of 1666.

Sam Smith's have been brewing in Tadcaster since 1758. And yes, Tadcaster's in North Yorkshire. No matter how many fine draught ales have come on the market since the turn of the 21st century, I always imagine that there are Yorkshiremen licking the froth from their lips before proclaiming, "I don't care what tha' says, there's nowt better than Sam's".

In their London pubs (around fifteen at the last count) you can have any beer you like as long as it's Sam's. That goes for the lager and the stout as well as the bitter. I once saw off a formidable yet tender steak pie at the Windsor Castle with the Extra Stout. At £3.40 a pint, it was 50p more than the Old Brewery Bitter.

Closing Time

Yes, that's right. Two pounds ninety for a well-kept pint, brewed in Tadcaster and served up in a pub restored to its Victorian prime and not far from Victoria Station.

I don't care what "tha' says"; in London there's "nowt" cheaper than Sam's.

* * * *

We can't leave London without mentioning the Fox and Hounds in SW1 and the Royal Oak in SE1. That's Tabard Street, SE1, not far from the 14th century Tabard tavern on Borough High Street where Geoffrey Chaucer's chums gathered before setting off on their pilgrimage to Canterbury.

The Royal Oak in Tabard Street offering the chance to savour the distinctive taste of Harvey's ales after a short walk from London Bridge Station

4 - To London via Lancaster

Framed extracts from his *Canterbury Tales* are spread around the walls of the upstairs function room of the Royal Oak. And a portrait of the author hangs above a sofa in the back bar that is one of the few concessions to comfort in an unspoilt street-corner boozer of the old school. Plenty of hard wooden settles and stools are available to perch on while admiring the decorative etched glass set into more dark wood behind the bar.

There's even a little hatchway where, as I mused in the Pint to Pint column, "jugs of ale may once have passed through in the days when it was all pie-and-eel shops round here".

The ale today is Harvey's, brewed in Lewes "dahn sarf" since 1790, as the engraved windows encased in mellowed yellow London brick remind passers-by. The Sussex Best suited me just fine as one who had developed a taste for that hoppily complex bitter on visits to see the Brighton branch of our family.

Unusually for such a southerly brewery, Harvey's also produce a dark mild. It's only three percent alcohol by volume yet mellow and rich in flavour. Went down a treat with my salt beef sandwich.

As for the Fox and Hounds in SW1, the local delicacies during my early-evening visit three or four years ago were Scotch eggs or pork pies. The latter came with a knife and some English mustard.

Dijon? A tossed salad? Where do you think we were: Belgravia?

Well, yes, believe it or not. This unspoiled street-corner pub was surrounded by exceedingly expensive housing. It served a pint of Young's that was far from "ordinary" and offered the chance to chat in cosy corners bordered by weathered settles or at a bar where, as long-time landlady Dee Dean confided, "you might find a street cleaner talking to a high-court judge".

And it was not unknown to hear actors from the nearby Royal Court holding forth.

Yes, *the* Royal Court on Sloane Square, the theatre that had developed a reputation for staging cutting-edge drama ever since John Osborne's *Look Back in Anger* had first set off ructions among the "chattering classes" in 1956.

In those days another writer who would make something of a name for himself lived close to the Fox and Hounds in what was then a run-down, sooty terrace largely populated by servants of the Grosvenor Estate. His name was Tony Warren and his first television script "Our Street" was rejected by the BBC. No doubt it was considered somewhat downmarket. Too working-class, old boy.

Warren duly changed the name and location to his native Salford. Then he sold the idea to Granada TV. The rest is history. By gum, it's a rum thought that he might have had elements of the Fox and Hounds on Passmore Street, Belgravia, in mind while creating scenes in the Rovers Return, Coronation Street.

Chapter Five

Goose Fair Peas and a Pint of "Shippo's"

Nottingham had hosted a Goose Fair since the Middle Ages. Once a place to sell geese brought waddling into town by farmers from far and wide, it evolved into an enormous funfair selling everything from candyfloss to brandy-snaps, hot dogs to mushy peas.

The peas were served in a carton. With mint sauce, if you please. And that remained a delicacy in many a local pub. Not just when the fair was lighting up the Forest recreation ground in the first week of October, but all the year round.

As for "Shippo's" in the chapter title above, that was the local name for Shipstone's, one of three Nottinghamshire breweries that had remained beyond the clutches of the big, keg-spreading conglomerates. So far. All three supplied their outlets predominantly with draught beer, or "real ale" as it was becoming known in the early seventies.

Shipstone's was based at Basford in the inner-city and Home Brewery at Daybrook, to the north of the city and close to Arnold where Jackie and I finally secured a mortgage on our first house in 1973.

The other local brewery was Hardys' and Hanson's, otherwise known as Kimberley. That's where it was brewed, out west and slightly north of Nottingham in what might be termed "DH Lawrence country"– the Erewash Valley, in other words, full of men like Lawrence's father who'd worked up a decent thirst in hot and dusty conditions underground.

The H&H company chairman was one Colonel Thomas Forman Hardy and it just so happened that he'd inherited a newspaper as well as a brewery. The *Nottingham Evening Post* was where I'd landed a job as feature writer at the end of 1972.

Feature articles gave you the opportunity to get behind the bare facts of news stories and put them in a wider context. They also gave you space to add some colour. Once established, I began to enjoy the job immensely. Then it became even better.

Out of the blue I was offered a regular column. "Pub Call", as it was dubbed, gave me the chance to chat to characters on both sides of the bar over a pint or two, listening to their stories and the histories of their "locals" while assessing the quality of the beer and the food. Yes, sometimes there was more on offer than Goose Fair peas.

By then I'd become used to men as well as women calling me "duck" or greeting me with "eyup, me duck". That was what you might call standard Nottingham-ese.

I'd also learnt to ask for a "cob" for lunch, rather than a "roll" or a "bap". The so-called Queen of the Midlands had a distinctive dialect of its own. I was growing to like the place. Returning to London could wait for a while.

Apart from anything else, our first child was on the way.

* * * *

Nottingham's reputation for draught beer went back quite a way. The sandstone caves below many an inn or tavern enabled publicans to keep their casks of ale at a constant temperature, winter or summer, long before the coming of cellar cooling systems. Hence the old song:

> *Nottingham ale, boys, Nottingham ale,*
> *No liquor on earth is like Nottingham ale.*
> *If she takes a glass often, there's nothing will soften*
> *The heart of a woman like Nottingham ale.*

Written in pre-feminist days, needless to say. And anyone who took a glass of Shippo's too often would have been well advised to go easy on the peas. Four pints and a carton could well bring a fart on.

5 - Goose Fair Peas and a Pint of "Shippo's"

Shipstone's was perhaps the most distinctive of the three Nottingham ales. Its bitter was dry, complex and heavily hopped. There was nothing wrong with it when it left Basford, as I could testify having once been granted a much-coveted tour of that brewery. But back then not all licensees seemed to have been trained in keeping it in peak condition.

As I wrote in *Britain's Lost Breweries and Beers*, "when it was good it was very, very good but when it was bad it was horrid. Or, as Dickens rather than Longfellow might have observed, 'It was the best of beers; it was the worst of beers'."

One Friday evening I recall being in a Shipstone's pub in Stapleford on the west side of the city. It was full of men who'd done a hot and hard week's labour at the nearby Stanton Iron Works, then part of British Steel. They saw off pint after pint while I was spacing out each unsavoury sip. To me it seemed far too sharp – Shippo's at its worst.

And Shippo's at its best?

Three distant memories have just sprung to mind. One was the St Ann's Inn, a somewhat soulless building in the '60s Shipstone tradition of a red-brick exterior with red Rexine seats inside. It had a sizeable car-park, mind you, and was an easy walk to and from the city centre. The landlord let me park there all day for nothing. He also kept a very acceptable pint of bitter. And mild. Plenty of that went down to sooth the locals' vocals during Saturday-night sing-songs.

St Ann's was by then a council estate on the site of what had been a sizeable slum until comparatively recently. And as I witnessed first-hand on more than one occasion, there was still appalling slum housing across town at The Meadows – an idyllic name for a setting where grass and flowers were in short supply.

At least those terrible terraces were finally being transformed into another big council estate by the long, dry summer of 1976 when I found myself walking back from a Test match at Trent Bridge. I'd just filed a feature about the lively West Indies fans who were an enjoyable part of the game in those days.

It was hot. Very hot. A fearsome thirst was raging by the time I reached the top of Arkwright Street and a pub called the Queen's came into view like a mirage. Its full title was the Queen's Hotel. Maybe it offered rooms for visitors arriving at the nearby mainline station. All I remember after that long trudge from Trent Bridge is quenching my thirst in a basic bar with a sublime pint of Shippo's.

It was up there with the bitter in the Turf Tavern at the time. And believe me, that was praise indeed.

The Turf was just round the corner from the *Evening Post* and opposite the Theatre Royal. For about three years, from the mid '70s onwards, it was run by a delightful couple called Jim and Doreen. Can't remember their surnames, but I can remember Jim's impeccable cellar-keeping. The Shipstone's was as good as it looked. You could see it gleaming clearly in a glass cylinder before an electric switch on the side sent it gushing into your glass.

While savouring the first swallow you might look up to see cigarette smoke swirling in occasional shafts of sunlight as they illuminated elaborately etched windows.

Conversations would be broken by bursts of laughter as hacks swapped yarns with amiable locals and, occasionally, theatricals from near and far. Sometimes we might even pick up a story or two.

On the way to and from the office we'd walk past the Peach Tree. It had been immortalised by Nottingham-born novelist Alan Sillitoe as one of the haunts of Arthur Seaton, the womaniser and sinker of many a pint in *Saturday Night and Sunday Morning*.

Nearly twenty years on from the book's first publication the Peach Tree's beer offer was Whitbread's "Big Head" Trophy Bitter, pumped full of gas to provide lots of froth. Or to put it another way, "all piss and wind, like a barber's cat".

That's a quote from a "customer in a Midlands pub commenting on keg beer". And I'm quoting it from a book that made a big impression on me at the time. It was called *The Death of the English Pub*.

A somewhat premature prediction, perhaps, published as it was in 1973. But it seemed like a shrewd analysis of the way the Big Six brewing conglomerates were maximising their profits while ruining our locals and the beers they served.

The author was Christopher Hutt who would go on to become an early national chairman of the Campaign for Real Ale. And Camra would go on to become the most successful of consumer pressure groups.

A small example of how things have changed is the aforesaid Peach Tree. Last time I looked in it was a pleasant enough free house called Langtry's, offering a wide range of real ales.

And The Turf?

That seems to have been through all kinds of manifestations since Jim and Doreen's departure. But not long before the lockdown it had been taken over by the licensee of the Johnson Arms near the city's main hospital -- another pub offering well-kept real ales a-plenty. One was from a micro-brewery in nearby Basford called, er, Shipstone's.

* * * *

Time, perhaps, to move on to Home Brewery. More specifically, to a city-centre pub that provided what might be termed a Home service. Of sorts. The service could be somewhat acerbic at the Peacock on Mansfield Road when licensee Maurice Oldham was summoned by one of the electric bell pushes.

Closing Time

Each table had a bell behind it. They were ranged around a lounge bar blessed with some distinctive engraved windows of peacocks in full feather and an aquarium of exotic fish in full fin.

Distinctive windows upstairs and down at the Peacock

My old friend John Holmes, long-time presenter on BBC Radio Nottingham as well as being a Radio Four producer, recalled being in there one lunch-time when a newcomer wandered in. He appeared somewhat baffled by the absence of a bar. "Just press a bell," John advised him. "It's waiter service."

"That's posh," the newcomer replied before finding a seat, pressing a bell and waiting. And waiting. So he pressed again. Maurice's head almost immediately shot out of the doorway at the far end of the room and bawled, "Bloody wait".

Eventually, and somewhat grudgingly, mine host appeared at the newcomer's table where he received a tentative request for a pint of bitter. And when that was finally delivered, there was another request: "Do you have any rolls?"

5 - Goose Fair Peas and a Pint of "Shippo's"

"We call 'em cobs," Maurice barked back. "And we've only got cheese and onion."

Having taken the money, he headed back to the doorway and the till beyond. Then his head shot out into the lounge again as if he'd just remembered something. "The cobs are in that perspex case," he growled. "You've got legs, haven't you?"

In those days the Peacock was very much a second home for Radio Nottingham employees. After all, the studios were just across the road. Another good friend, Allister Craddock, was a producer there before moving into television. He still harbours many a memory of Maurice – particularly the time that he tripped on his way from the bar to the lounge and "parted company" with a tray of drinks:

"One moment a nearby customer was innocently reading his paper, the next he was dripping with Home Bitter while his paper had suddenly turned into papier mâché. "Such was the power of Maurice's glare that his victim blurted 'I'm sorry'."

But there was another side to the man dubbed the "rudest landlord in Britain" by the late Frank Palmer, East Midland correspondent for the *Daily Mirror*, when Maurice and his wife Edie bade farewell to the Peacock and went off to live in Australia.

As Allister recalled, "beneath the rude exterior was another surly interior and below that a softer version that Maurice occasionally revealed when his guard was down".

He certainly revealed it to me on one of my early visits to the Peacock. We were in the public bar and I'd somehow become engaged in a game of darts with two Australians. Maybe they were here for a Test match at Trent Bridge.

Sips of Home bitter between throws seemed particularly lip-smacking on that occasion and Maurice chatted amiably while topping them up. Even handed me a "cob" from the Perspex container.

Closing Time

But by then he knew that I was researching a piece for the *Pub Call* column.

* * * *

The Home Brewery bitter was even better, or at least more consistent, at a pub not too far down the road and round the corner from the Peacock in Lower Parliament Street. Built in 1929, it is now the Newmarket offering "live bands and DJs six nights a week". At least it was pre-lockdown. Back in the '70s it was the New Market (two words) offering oddball conversations.

Locked door at the Newmarket

The landlord, Tony Green, was something of an oddball himself. His nickname "Dodger" had been acquired during his days in the local police force. Certainly he seemed to revel in dodging the obligation to wear a uniform since moving from PC to licensee.

5 - Goose Fair Peas and a Pint of "Shippo's"

Allister Craddock, whom we met in the Peacock [see above], remembered Dodger making his entrance to the New Market sporting "khaki military shorts and wellies with a knowingly mischievous expression. He always delighted in the absurd."

Had a dog called Muffin for whom he bought a season ticket at Notts County FC. BBC television's *Football Focus* featured Dodger and dog heading for the Meadow Lane ground one Saturday. By bike. Muffin was pictured peeping out of the saddle bag.

Like one or two licensees that I mentioned earlier, Tony seemed determined to keep pre-decimal "old money" in circulation. "He drove his local bank mad with his demand for bags of sixpences," Allister reminded me. "And we felt duty bound to do our best to keep them in circulation"

Allister also remembered being in the lounge bar, otherwise known "the best side", one evening with "a leading solicitor talking to the manager of the local sauna alongside the president of the Agricultural Workers' Union, John Hose, and John McNeil who'd just driven his train back from St Pancras".

Pictures of steam railways adorned the lounge bar walls – a treat for train buff and actor Phil Jackson, otherwise known as Chief Inspector Japp in in Agatha Christie's *Poirot* and for many another TV and film role. John Holmes had interviewed him on Radio Nottingham before escorting him to the New Market where, on seeing those steamy photos, he proclaimed himself "to be in heaven".

And that was before he'd had a pint.

The draught beer was dispensed by handpumps, something of a rarity in those days when electric pumps (or carbon dioxide) tended to transfer ale from cellar to glass. Maybe that's why the Nottingham branch of Camra gathered in the New Market's public bar at regular intervals.

Closing Time

Before we leave the New Market, I should just mention the cosy back room where I held two leaving "dos" in the early 1980s – one from the *Nottingham News* and the other from Radio Nottingham where I, too, was briefly a producer. Only after a turbulent time, mind you, in my somewhat unconventional journalistic career.

* * * *

As I mentioned earlier, Colonel Forman Hardy was the chairman of the *Nottingham Evening Post* as well as well as Hardys' and Hanson's Brewery in Kimberley. He had inherited both and liked to project himself as a somewhat paternalistic figure. Most years he would send his journalists a cash bonus for Christmas along with a letter passing on seasonal greetings to our "wives and sweethearts".

Yet he had appointed as his managing director a lofty character called Christopher Pole-Carew. Not only was he exceedingly tall; he also looked down with disdain on trade unions. When the National Union of Journalists called a nationwide strike at the end of 1978, anyone who left their desk was threatened with instant dismissal. Around a dozen walked out anyway. And when Pole-Carew followed up on his threat, I was one of sixteen who felt strongly that the sackings were unjust.

We duly joined our colleagues on the picket line and we too were locked out. For good. "The Nottingham twenty eight", as we became labelled, were the only NUJ members not to be allowed back to our desks when the strike came to an end.

None of us drank Kimberley Ales for a while after that. Not at the brewery tap, the Nelson and Railway, where I remember spending a convivial Sunday evening for a *Pub Call* column along with my genial if somewhat bibulous "chauffeur", Stewart Argyle, another real ale loving former policeman. Nor even at the Lord Nelson, a pub that seemed to belong to a rural village but had somehow been planted in inner-city Sneinton.

5 - Goose Fair Peas and a Pint of "Shippo's"

"It had probably been a farm-house or a cottage, converted into a pub in the nineteenth century," mused Dave Ablitt, another old friend from Nottingham days who met his future wife Judy there in 1969. "The building was beamed with quite a few rooms and a nice garden. Eric Smith was the licensee in those days and he never sold crisps. Didn't want them littering up his tables."

Standards slipped somewhat during the '80s, I'm told. But the Nelson seemed to have made something of a comeback since then. And hopefully it will come back again post-lockdown.

* * * *

Talking of comebacks, I should mention the Hand and Heart across town from Sneinton and close to Canning Circus where the roads to Derby, Ilkeston and Alfreton converge. It was also next door to the derelict building in which we established the *Nottingham News* in the wake of our sacking from the *Evening Post*.

Thankfully, the journalists' union was paying us the same net salary as we'd been earning at the *Post*. But as one with a wife, two children and another on the way, I was very conscious of the need to land a more permanent job. In the meantime, beer money needed to be a little on the tight side. Any lunchtime pints (very much part of journalism at the time) would have to be made to last.

That wasn't too difficult at the Hand and Heart. The Shipstone's was sharp and not exactly more-ish. And the surroundings could best be described as basic. The pub was built into one of those aforementioned sandstone caves but no effort had been made to show it off.

Fast forward to 2015 and the place had not only made a comeback; it had been transformed. The front bar was lined with no fewer than eight handpumps dispensing beers from small breweries in and around Nottingham. I finally settled on one from Dancing Duck, based sixteen miles up the road in Derby, having been assured by the barmaid that it was "well-rounded".

Round Heart, as it was aptly called, went down a treat with a lunch of melt-in-the-mouth beef in a rich red wine sauce. Mushrooms and slivers of carrot bobbed up from the bowl, chased around by chunks of ciabatta bread. Jackie was equally enthusiastic about her belly pork in cider sauce.

And we weren't even in the restaurant. We were sitting not far from a piano that the barmaid assured me burst into life on Sundays under the fingers, and sometimes the toes, of a pianist known as "Pete the Feet".

As for the more formal dining area, that was in the cave beyond, now lit up like a fairy grotto. I assured readers of the *Telegraph*'s *Pint to Pint* column that "the sandstone is brushed twice a week to prevent gritty grains from falling into their confit of duck or 'slow-braised' oxtail".

* * * *

Perhaps the city's best known pub was also built into a cave – the one crested by what's left of Nottingham Castle. Whoever ran the Trip to Jerusalem in the 1970s didn't take quite so much trouble over brushing down the sandstone as they did at the Hand and Heart in 2015. I distinctly remember being in what might be called the cliff-drop bar with a pint of Ruddle's County, a much-treasured beer among real-ale buffs in those days.

The appeal of that particular pint began to wane, however, when I glanced down and noticed several gritty bits floating around on its flattish head. After pointing this out, I received some sound advice from a regular sitting nearby: "Tha' should always put a beer mat on top of your glass between swigs in 'ere, youth."

Well, I was a young man in those days and "youth" was another Nottingham dialect term for just about anyone below forty.

As for the Trip – or "Ye Olde" Trip to Jerusalem as it was inevitably labelled – that has been through many manifestations since we left

5 - Goose Fair Peas and a Pint of "Shippo's"

Nottingham. And in recent times it had become a pleasure to revisit. But the sign on the side claiming this to to be "the oldest inn in England" is somewhat dubious. So is the date, 1189. That just happened to be when Richard the Lionheart came to the throne. Yes, his army once besieged his brother John at Nottingham Castle on a brief break from the crusades, but I somehow doubt that they called in for a pint or even a cup of sac.

The Trip may not even be the oldest pub in Nottingham. "Ye Olde" Salutation on nearby Hounds Gate would contend the claim. It has parts dating back to 1240, even though it now stands close to a somewhat soulless dual carriageway and the "Sal" had become well known locally for its rock music nights BC (Before Corona).

A Channel 4 documentary made in 1998 diplomatically decreed that the Salutation was housed in the oldest building and the Trip had the oldest caves below and around it.

And the oldest pub?

That was said to be the Bell Inn on Angel Row with its restored stained glass and flag-stoned central passageway.

The Bell stands close to the Old Market Square and opposite another Grade II listed building. It was designed as an ornate gin palace in the 1880s with an extravagantly decorative frontage and many a marble statue ranged around the interior.

By the 1970s it had become a branch of Yates's Wine Lodge. The speciality of the house was Australian wine. Not the Chardonnays, Sauvignon Blancs, Shirazes or Merlots that line the shelves of many a British supermarket today, but something unspeakably sweet that gushed from one or another of many barrels lining the back of the bar.

"Draught Champagne" was a speciality of the Blackpool branch. But calling for a bottle of "champers" caused quite a stir in the Nottingham Yates's, as I recall all too well when I ventured in with Frank Palmer, the East Midlands correspondent of the *Mirror* whom I briefly mentioned with regard to the Peacock (see above).

Frank was a generous man, always happy to share his lavish expenses. The barman, however, did not seem impressed. "Champagne?" he muttered, shaking his head before trudging off towards the cellar. Eventually he re-emerged with a dusty bottle that he banged on the bar with evident irritability.

Frank then had the audacity to ask for an ice bucket. After more head-shaking, something that looked more like a plastic coal bucket appeared on the bar with a few cubes already melting amid the black dust. "Will that do ya'?" grumped the barman.

It had to.

Yes, there was keg beer available. Many of the trilbied regulars didn't seem too bothered that it wasn't real ale. They saw off plenty of it while chatting up one or more of the peroxide blondes that also tended to gravitate to Yates's.

You had to keep your eye open for disputes. Fisticuffs were not unknown, even on those evenings when a trio in faded dinner jackets were sawing away at stringed instruments on the balustrade balcony above.

The late Emrys Bryson, long-time theatre critic at the *Post* and a much-admired writer, once described the local Yates's as "a mixture of palm court and Wild West". And in his *Portrait of Nottingham*, published by Robert Hale and Co in 1974, he recounted the following tale:

"The Victorian owner of what was once Yates's Wine Lodge used to be very fond of marble statuary, which he scattered around the premises. At closing time one night, an extremely tanked-up patron was accidentally locked in, slumped beneath a table. He regained

5 - Goose Fair Peas and a Pint of "Shippo's"

consciousness in the deserted bar to the sight of the moon glimmering eerily on the white figures.

"From that moment, Nottingham ale lost one of its best customers."

* * * *

David Lowe, another friend from the features department at the *Post*, more recently edited the paper's Bygones section. As the name suggests, it looked back to the "good old days" – the "good old days" of Nottingham's pubs in the case of an evocative piece by John Brunton in an edition from April, 2000.

Ah yes, the good old days when you could only be served in the lounge or "best side" if you were dressed smartly. The good old days when women were barely tolerated in some bars and not at all in the "gents only". The good old days when cigarette smoke clogged the air, the draught beer varied from the sublime to the "gor blimey" and the main food offer (apart from Goose Fair peas) amounted to crisps or pickled eggs.

Memories of pickled eggs surfaced when I found myself back in Arnold for the first time in nigh-on forty years. Yes, Arnold where we'd bought our first house and had our first child. Thumbing through the *Telegraph*'s book of *Pint to Pint* columns, I see that I described the Robin Hood and Little John on Church Street as "a shrine to the traditional street-corner 'boozer'".

Except that it offered more. Much more. The pickled eggs were labelled "free-range and locally sourced". Unlike their eye-wateringly acidic predecessors from the "good old days", the one that I sampled didn't give the impression that it had spent several years in the jar.

The jar shared a bar with an espresso machine, forty-four whiskies from around the globe and eight draught ciders. As for the draught beers, there was an extensive range from Lincoln Green, one of heaven knows how many micro-breweries to have sprung up in Nottingham and elsewhere since the turn of the century.

I'd finally settled on the Hood, a perfectly balanced bitter that brought back memories of Home at its best. Home Brewery, that is, brewed up the road in Daybrook until was been taken over by the late-but-not-lamented Scottish and Newcastle in 1986.

Shipstone's had been swallowed up by Greenall Whitley towards the end of the '70s and finally closed down in 1991. And Hardys' and Hanson's had sold out to Greene King in June, 2006. The brewery was closed that December.

The biggest brewer in Nottingham today is Castle Rock, founded by Chris Holmes, an old drinking mate of mine from the days when he was a lecturer at what was then the Trent Polytechnic. He became national chairman of Camra in 1975 before opening his first pub, the King's Arms in Newark, two years later. It wouldn't be the last.

Chris Holmes opening his first pub in Newark in 1977

5 - Goose Fair Peas and a Pint of "Shippo's"

Chris and I still meet up now and again, usually at a Trent Bridge Test Match. Three of Castle Rock's twenty four outlets stand nearby. One of them is the Embankment, incorporating a bar called the Dispensary. Well, this was once the social club of Boots the Chemist and Boots had begun in Nottingham where its founder was born and brought up. Sir Jesse Boot's wood-panelled office has been immaculately restored as a function room.

The Dispensary dispenses a veritable array of real ales from Castle Rock as well as guest beers from elsewhere. (I've written that in the present tense in the hope that it will be open to the public, along with cricket grounds, one of these days.)

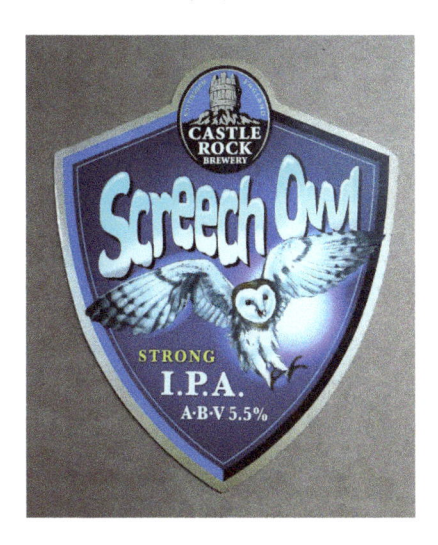

A popular ale from Castle Rock

Embankment and Dispensary stand just across the river from the Trent Bridge ground. The Brewery Tap, otherwise known as the Vat and Fiddle stands conveniently close to the station and indeed the building that once housed the Queen's Hotel. That ambrosial pint of Shippo's bitter that I recall so well from '76 would have been one of two options back then. The other was Shippo's mild.

The choice is somewhat wider at the Vat. Around seven of the draught beers on offer are from the brewery that towers over this 1930s Art Deco-style pub. Guest beers, too, needless to say.

Duly fortified by one or another, I would stroll on to catch a Birmingham-bound train. Sometimes I might get off at Beeston, just one stop west of the city centre, and stay overnight with our youngest daughter Elizabeth and her family.

No, I wouldn't go out for any more drinks. But should I wish to, there used to be four or five pubs within walking distance. Hopefully all will reopen when these viral times are behind us. They serve an abundance of impeccably kept real ale, most from local breweries.

Very different from some forty years ago when Liz was born nearby and, eventually, I took friends out to wet her head with a pint or two of Shipstone's that had somehow lost its hoppy, bitter edge since the Greenall takeover.

The "good old days", eh?

Chapter Six

Batches and Bass in the City of Culture[s]

Forty years on and I can still remember my first lunchtime in the Town Wall Tavern in Bond Street. No, not that Bond Street. This was Bond Street, Coventry, just round the corner from the Belgrade Theatre's stage door and overlooking an expansive (and expensive) car park.

The Town Wall Tavern, one time haven of the hacks

It was my second day as features editor of the nearby *Evening Telegraph*. The first lunchbreak had largely been spent going between the car park over the road and the police station on the other side of the city centre. I'd driven fifty miles from Nottingham that morning to be in time for the editorial conference at 8.15 and somehow managed to lock my ignition key inside. Don't ask how. Maybe I was half asleep. Anyway, the policeman who arrived with a set of keys to rival those of the chief prison officer at Pentonville eventually found one that opened the door.

It was July 20, 1981 – a momentous day for cricket-lovers, of which I'm one. Ian Botham scored a buccaneering hundred-and-forty-nine not out against Australia to give England a chance of winning the Headingley Test match against all odds.

The stage was set for a memorable July 21. Enter an almost dementedly focused Bob Willis on a small black-and-white television that licensee Ray Hoare had rigged up behind the bar at the Town Wall. It was day five at Headingley, day two for me at the *Telegraph* and day one at the Wall.

There would be more days and nights. Many more. But few would be quite as noisy. Willis took most of his eight wickets during my late lunchbreak and the hubbub grew. One voice soared above all the others, however, once I'd finally made it through the crowd around the bar. "What d'ya want?" bawled the barmaid.

Joan was her name and, as I would later discover, bawling was second nature to her, even on days when the public bar was less crowded. "Joan of Bark," I would later christen her. But first I would have to answer her question after surveying the handpumps and fleetingly wondering if I was back in Birmingham.

Mitchell's and Butler's Brew XI?

No thanks.

Draught Bass?

Tempting, but a perhaps a little on the strong side for lunchtime.

So I settled on M&B Springfield bitter. Brewed in Wolverhampton in those days, it was comparatively light on alcohol and less cloying than the Brew.

6 - Batches and Bass in the City of Culture[s]

"Have you got a cheese cob to go with it?" I bawled back at Joan as a roar greeted yet another Willis wicket.

"What's a cob?" she enquired in a voice that could have been heard in Nottingham.

To cut a long story short, I discovered that here in Coventry they called rolls "batches". I would also discover an alternative for lunchtimes to come – the substantial and extremely tasty pies cooked up by Ray's wife Jo and delivered by his mother, a woman with a Cockney accent and a voice almost as loud as Joan of Bark's. "Mind your backs!" was her piercing pie cry as she barged her way through journalists, stage-hands and thespians thronging the main bar with its cosy open fire at one end and etched glass windows at the other.

The building dates back to 1825 and between bar and lounge there remains to this day one of the smallest snugs in all England, measuring seven foot eight inches by five foot five. Bar stools only in there. One was the perching place of Barrie Clark, editor of a freesheet known as the *Coventry Citizen*. An amiably bow-tied if somewhat crumpled figure, Barrie had a prodigious capacity for Bass and a squawking laugh that threatened to shatter the door glass engraved with the words "Donkey Box".

The entry to the the Donkey Box snug a the Town Wall

The snug had been dubbed with that name since a donkey joined the cast at a Belgrade panto and someone from the theatre had the bright idea, between rehearsals, of seeing if it would fit into the snug.

It did. Just about.

That was a bit before my time at the *Telegraph* and heaven knows what Ray had to say about it. He could be an abrasive figure at times. Rugby supporters were welcome. Round-ball football fans were not. Anyone sporting football paraphernalia would be pointed towards the front door on the assumption, presumably, that they were all potential hooligans. Above the back door to the toilets, meanwhile, was a sign saying "Students' Entrance".

Fast forward four decades and the Town Wall is now dwarfed by blocks of student apartments spread across that long-gone car park. Coventry has become very much an academic hub. Warwick University lies within its boundaries and Coventry University takes up an increasingly large part of the city centre.

It seemed very different back in the early '80s. What had once been a great manufacturing centre had been labelled a "ghost town". By the Specials, needless to say, the most successful band on the 2-Tone label that had been spawned in the city in the late '70s. *Ghost Town* was number one in the charts on the week that I started at the *Telegraph*.

Car factories were shedding workers or closing down completely. Obituaries for the city were being penned in national newspapers. Not for the first time, I might add.

At least the local newspaper was thriving under the editorship of Geoff Elliott. Word had spread that *Coventry Evening Telegraph* was a haven for fearless local journalism, and many budding national newspaper writers, broadcasters and television presenters were learning their craft in a noisy newsroom still clattering with typewriters.

6 - Batches and Bass in the City of Culture[s]

By that time I was in my early thirties with a wife and three small children. It took a while to get the family settled in Coventry, but I remain grateful to Geoff for giving me a chance to get back into newspapers – not only running a department on a decent salary but writing two regular columns.

One was largely made up of my personal reflections on the news, local and national. The other was called "Pubscrawl", a variation on the title of its equivalent in the Nottingham papers. The "scrawl" part, I might add, had nothing to do with my attempts to decipher shorthand notes the morning after visiting a hostelry anywhere from the inner-city to rural Warwickshire.

Sunday lunch offerings at the Town Wall Tavern

I researched the column in my own time and over time it made me warm towards a place that would eventually evolve from "Ghost Town" to the 2021 UK City of Culture. I began to realise that it had long been a city of cultures, full of people from somewhere else with good stories to tell.

Needless to say, the Town Wall was an early entrant in the Pubscrawl slot. The place had been a godsend when I'd first arrived in Coventry and remained so forty years on.

There has been many a licensee since Ray's departure. One was Martin McKeown who cooked a lobster that some joker had sent me in the post. Another (briefly) was Jim Holton, former Manchester United, Coventry City and Scotland centre-back – a much more sociable bloke off the field than on. Jim died at a tragically early age a few years later.

Yet another was former restaurateur Lesley Jackson. Lesley and her partner came up with pies even more exotic than those cooked by Ray's wife and delivered by his mum. Among them were mutton cobbler and rabbit crumble. The contents of both had a surprisingly melt-in-the-mouth tenderness about them.

Jackie and I used to head for the Wall on our way to the Belgrade or, more often, the nearby Odeon. At least we did until the lockdown. Hopefully we will again in the not too distant future. No mutton or rabbit on more recent occasions, but traditional English pub grub expertly cooked by a chef of African-Caribbean origin.

As for the draught beer, it was kept in tip-top condition. Plenty more choice these days, sometimes including very tempting Adnam's Best, all the way from our much-loved Southwold. But the Bass mirror glimmering next to that open fire in the bar was a reminder of the ale that still took some beating here. As well kept, I might add, as it was in Ray's day.

And that's praise indeed.

* * * *

During the Middle Ages Coventry was one of the four most important English cities outside London. But on November 14, 1940, much of its mediaeval core was destroyed by German bombs.

6 - Batches and Bass in the City of Culture[s]

As if that wasn't enough, the Luftwaffe returned in April the following year for another blitz. Factories that had once pioneered the production of bikes, motorbikes and motorcars had by then become significant players in making munitions. Hence the bombing and hence the need for widespread rebuilding.

The Old Windmill - "Ma Brown,s" - in Spon Street

Some of the mediaeval survivors were moved from their original locations to be reassembled in half-timbered rows on either side of a single street – Spon Street, to be precise, between the country's first pedestrian precinct and part of the new ring road that encircled the city with cars, many of which had been built locally.

The Old Windmill had not needed to be reassembled, however. It was a blitz survivor that had stood on Spon Street for several centuries. Indeed the open stone hearth in the main bar once harboured a priest hole. Beyond is another room containing restored remnants of the built-in brew-house, dating back to the early 1930s when the pub was surrounded by courtyards of terraced housing.

Older Coventrians still refer to the Windmill as "Ma Brown's". She was the redoubtable landlady who took over after the death in 1940 of her husband Sydney, a former coffin-maker. Ma ruled the bar until her death in 1967. Or "bars", I should day. To this day there are three snugs off a polished passageway of well-worn stone.

One of them has red and black tiles and a black-leaded stove that looks as though it once simmered many a stew. On Sunday lunchtimes in Ma's day it would have been full of local women shelling peas or peeling carrots while seeing off a "dogs' nose" or two. That was, apparently, a gin with half a bitter (not necessarily in the same glass).

The snug across the passageway has an open fire, a shelf lined with books and a hatchway to the main bar. Between the two is the snuggest of snugs bordered by a gleaming brass counter.

I've written the last three paragraphs in the present tense in the fervent hope that this handsome hostelry will reopen come the day in mid-May when mingling inside public, not just private houses, is finally allowed. As I write, that's still two and a half months away.

I'm also fervently hoping that Michelle Gilmour will still be the licensee. "The Ma Brown de nos jours," I called her in *Pint to Pint*. Looking back through a book of those columns, I see that this one appeared in the *Sunday Telegraph* in 2015. Michelle was only thirty at the time, yet she had a real feeling for the traditional pub. Darts, dominoes and crib teams were made welcome.

The food offer was pork pie, pork pie or pork pie. Very good pork pie, mind you, from a stall on the nearby market. As for the beer offer from a long line of handpumps, that was infinitely better than it had been when I'd first blown into the Windmill back in the '80s.

6 - Batches and Bass in the City of Culture[s]

One of them was Theakston's Old Peculier (with an 'e', not an 'a'), an old favourite of those with a taste for complex, dark and powerful ales that roll soothingly over the tongue. But my favourite was another Yorkshire product: Timothy Taylor's Landlord, a robust bitter that, at the time, was served straight from a barrel in the cellar.

It was later granted a handpump of its own, which at least gave it a proper Yorkshire head. No gin required for a "dog's nose", thanks all the same.

* * * *

Shortly we shall be heading over or under the ring road (via subway or pelican crossing) from Spon Street to Spon End. The "Spon End Run", as it used to be known in the '80s and '90s, was a popular "pub crawl" involving pubs and publicans of character. The "run" included the adjacent terraced streets of Chapelfields where watchmaking had been the staple trade a century or so previously.

First, though, let's nip across the city centre to another blitz survivor that could claim, like Ma Brown's, the title 'oldest inn in town'. The Golden Cross, half-timbered and leaded-windowed, was built "circa 1583". That's what it says on a plaque on the handsome exterior. Another plaque points out that it was "best music pub" winner in 2005.

There was still music upstairs until comparatively recently, as I recall, but it was nowhere near as intrusive as it used to be when this was very much a haunt for students. The Cross's current owners had finally recognised its potential for a far wider market. They'd tried to make the most of the main downstairs room's surviving features following what the 2021 Good Beer Guide called "corporate vandalism in the 1960s".

Needless to say, the Cross wouldn't be in Camra's bible of bibulous havens were it not for a decent selection of well-kept real ales, often including the products of local breweries such as Byatt's and Church End. The lunchtime and early-doors evening meals weren't bad either.

And this splendid building on the corner of cobbled Hay Lane and Bayley Lane has at least two literary connections.

The Coventry Cross

JB Priestley stood outside the pub in the early '30s and marvelled at the "genuinely old and picturesque view". As he went on to write in *An English Journey* (1934), "You peep round a corner and see half-timbered buildings that would do for the second act of the Meistersinger. In fact, you could stage the second act of the Meistersinger – or film it – in Coventry."

6 - Batches and Bass in the City of Culture[s]

A survivor of the bombs

You still could. Admittedly what is now the "old" cathedral has lost its roof and much else since Priestley's day, but its haunting remains have staged many dramatic events, from mediaeval mystery plays to touring Shakespeare productions.

On the other side of Bayley Lane still stands the miraculous blitz survivor that is St Mary's Guildhall, where Henry VI and Margaret of Anjou briefly held court in the 1450s. Up the road and round the cobbled corner, meanwhile, stood the building that housed Coventry's central library until 1986.

Another literary figure, who just happened to be the son of the City Treasurer, spent much of his childhood and youth devouring books in there. As youth grew towards manhood, he would borrow books and lug them as far as the Golden Cross where he could browse over a pint while surreptitiously ogling the barmaid.

Philip Larkin would go to university in Oxford and finish up in Hull. But he was a "Coventry kid", to use the local term for those born and brought up in the city. (Not that that he would have used it about himself.)

Incidentally, the central library building that provided his reading material for the Golden Cross stood somewhere between the back of

Wilco's and the Old County Hall. A Grade II listed former courthouse and jail, the hall was built in 1783 and was the site of Britain's last public hanging.

More recently it had become a branch of the Slug and Lettuce pub chain.

* * * *

Never mind slugs and lettuce leaves; would anyone fancy a slice of steak and cow-heel pie? With mash and gravy, I should add.

No?

Believe me, you don't know what you're missing. Or "were" missing, I should say. The pie was an occasional plat du jour at the Old Dyers Arms in Spon End, the 1980s domain of Mavis Ogden.

Like her husband Barry, Mavis had come to Coventry from Oldham where heel-less cows were far more common. Or so I imagined. When I first tucked to one of those pies, I tried to put to the back of my mind a silly vision of cattle limping over Lancashire fields and fells.

Mavis sported high heels. With low-cut dresses, what's more. On ladies' darts nights in particular, she strutted her stuff between throwing her arrows in a public bar full of characters of both sexes.

One was a called Len and could have stepped straight out of a Laurie Lee novel. He'd hold forth in a strong Gloucestershire accent and, I seem to recall, we had many a chat about cricket. When Radio-4's *Down Your Way* was due to come our way, one of the researchers asked me to recommend potential interviewees. And so it came to pass that Len was broadcast in conversation with the presenter at the time, one Brian Johnston who was better known for his commentaries on *Test Match Special*.

Can't remember what they discussed, or where they were. Not in the Dyers, I suspect. Otherwise Mavis may well have felt the need to interject and tell the BBC a few stories about the ghost that apparently plagued the pub in general and the cellar in particular.

The Old Dyers Arms where Mavis Ogden once reigned

The building dates back to the early 19th century and was originally called the Berkswell Tavern, after a Warwickshire village not far from Coventry. It became the Dyers in the 1840s.

Weaving and ribbon-making were part of Coventry's history and dyeing fabric of one kind or another went on regularly on the banks of the not-so-mighty Sherbourne. The river just happened to flow (or rather trickle) by on the other side of Spon End.

If memory serves, it made an appearance close to the back of the Malt Shovel, an ancient ale house across the road and fifty yards up from the Dyers. Still close enough to hear Mavis when she spotted me from an upstairs window and bawled, "You're going in the wrong pub."

Not a woman to argue with, Mrs Ogden. She now lives in Turkey and recently posted on Facebook a picture of a sumptuous Turkish meal that looked even more appetising than a steak and cowheel pie.

Don't ask me what food was served in the Malt Shovel in the '80s. What I do recall is a cosy beamed-and-brassed interior and draught beers that had come not just from Birmingham or Burton. Tetley's was part of the Allied Breweries conglomerate, along with Ansell's. A good sound Yorkshire bitter, it was still brewed in Leeds back then.

I remember savouring it while listening to folk sessions in the function room upstairs – finger-in-the ear folk on one occasion when unaccompanied soloists resurrected the songs of old England.

More often the songs of old Ireland pervaded pubs round here on certain evenings and weekend lunchtimes. In pre-Mavis days at the Dyers, I'm told, the back room would resound to the music of the Fureys. Davey Arthur apparently bedded down in a caravan in the pub's back garden before moving on to bigger things.

As for the Malt Shovel, it's now the site of a mind and body therapy centre. Sadly, it ceased to be a pub back in 2011.

* * * *

Closed, too, is another one-time Spon End gem. The building that housed the Black Horse still stands. Just about. It has been under threat of demolition for a road-widening scheme for as long as I can remember. So long that I vaguely recall fulminating against the threat when I was still writing a column in the local paper.

The licensees back then were Brendan and Bridie. Can't remember the surname but they were Irish, to be sure. Bridie kept a spotlessly clean tea towel on her shoulder. And when she wasn't pulling pints, she'd remove it with a flourish to polish glasses. "There you are, Pet," she'd say after filling a gleaming glass with a perfectly kept pint of Bass or thick and creamy draught Guinness.

6 - Batches and Bass in the City of Culture[s]

One-time domain of Brendan and Bridie - still awaiting demolition

Bridie never drank alcohol herself, mind you. Neither did Brendan when he was within her gaze at the Black Horse. But he'd take a break every now and then, telling his missus that he was going to walk the dog round the block. "Okay, Pet," she'd sigh.

Like a well-trained dray horse, the dog would wait patiently outside each pub that Brendan breezed into. When he emerged, his four-legged friend would stand up and move on.

Back at the Black Horse (eventually) Brendan might then join one of the distinctively Irish conversations that tended to take place in the cosy room beyond bar and lounge. A rum character called Des Tobin might be holding forth on any subject, from the Cheltenham racing festival to the works of James Joyce or WB Yeats.

Des was a literary man with good stories of his own to tell. Not a bad piano player either. A veteran of the Irish country dance circuit, he later tickled the ivories as one of the Sunday-lunchtime trio in the back room of the Earlsdon Cottage in the days of another legendary local licensee, Wal Haydon.

Hang on. We're getting ahead of ourselves. Earlsdon and Wal will come later. For now we're in Spon End, with Chapelfields still to come. Let's pop up the road a bit and turn left – a path often trodden by Brendan and his dog.

* * * *

Craven Street in Chapelfields was never short of licensed premises. Two clubs and four pubs pre-lockdown. Sorry, make that three. The Coombe Abbey, named after a somewhat grander building on the edge of the city, has been closed since 2015.

Thirty years previously it had been the scene of some revelry when Ireland won the Grand Slam in what was then the Five Nations rugby tournament. Landlord Pat McMahon was overjoyed and a framed photo of the winning side was duly hung on the wall of the cosy back room where folk musicians gathered to play tunes of Gaelic or Celtic origin.

As I mentioned in Chapter Two, Pat once drove me to the wilds of Norfolk for a bizarre evening at the Lord Nelson pub in Burnham Thorpe. Like Brendan from the much closer Black Horse (see above), he enjoyed being on the customers' side of the bar. And like Brendan, he had evidently been "a broth of a boy" in his youth.

For me the Coombe was a place to pop into on Sundays, usually for a pre-lunch pint in a convivial front bar. That was where I first met Alan Taylor who would later gaze into my eyes. Well, he was an optician. Sometimes I'd be in the back room on Sunday evenings, chatting (between tunes) to Pat or any number of old folkies.

Right next door to the Coombe is a pub of similar vintage. Mid 19th century, that is, when the lofts of the surrounding terraced houses

6 - Batches and Bass in the City of Culture[s]

would have housed watch-makers bent over the interiors of intricate tickers.

The Coombe (now closed) next to the thriving Hearsall

Times change in more ways than one. While the Coombe looked desolate last time I passed, the Hearsall Inn looked handsomely restored and (hopefully) ready to reopen come the hour, come the day. It had long taken over from its next-door neighbour as a haven of Irish music and English draught ale.

* * * *

Memories of all kinds of music came to mind when I strolled up the road to the Craven Arms and looked down Lord Street to the Nursery Tavern. Built on grounds that were once the nursery garden of Chapelfields House, it opened in the early 1860s.

Fast forward a hundred and twenty years and Mann's Brewery bought up the house next door. The pub duly doubled in size. Yet there was still an intimacy about the place pre-lockdown. Three distinctive rooms were linked by a lengthy bar offering selection of draught beers considerably tastier than Mann's.

To the right as you stepped through the front door was a half-timbered lounge, to the left a busier bar that used to rattle with chatter and the clatter of dominoes, and beyond a back room hosting everything from community meetings to music from a new generation of Coventrians.

A music session at the Nursery Tavern

The music would spill out on to a sizeable back terrace during the summer months. On a warmish evening you could be cradling a well-kept pint of Fuller's London Pride, listening to the one and only Wes Finch and glancing up every now and them to see lights glinting in lofts where watch-makers work no longer.

* * * *

Watch-making declined and motor manufacturing expanded as the twentieth century moved on. Farewell to small lofts, hello to big factories. Big pubs and clubs, too, built to accommodate thirsty workers who'd pile in at lunchtime or early evening.

6 - Batches and Bass in the City of Culture[s]

Many were to the north of the city centre, spread along the Foleshill Road and the Longford Road beyond. And most of those had closed and been converted into other uses long before lockdown.

The General Wolfe, with its ornate Edwardian frontage and fabled upstairs function room, closed ten years ago. Yet back in the late '70s and early '80s the place had been crammed with fans of any number of up-and-coming bands who played there, from U2 to the Eurythmics. Not forgetting local legends of the 2-Tone label, the Specials and the Selecter.

The General Wolfe

Foleshill Road and the streets around it have been largely populated by Asian families for many years. Further along from the Wolfe was the William IV, later renamed as Pele's Balti Pub.

The licensee had been a useful footballer in his youth. Hence the nickname. His real name was Perminder and, with his wife Jatinder, he launched Coventry's first curry pub.

Closing Time

It wouldn't be the last. The combination of well-cooked dishes with their origins in the sub-continent and M&B mild, with its origins at Cape Hill, near Smethwick, proved surprisingly seductive – for taste-buds and the tongue in my case.

Pele and Jatinder moved on long ago. Their former domain had become the JK Indian Restaurant last time that we passed en route for the Greyhound, a popular inn at Sutton Stop, Hawkesbury Junction, where the Oxford and Coventry canals come together. Not the easiest place to find once you've finally reached the northerly end of the Longford Road and looked in vain for a road sign. Well worth the effort, mind you.

The Greyhound at Sutton Stop at the junction of the Coventry and Oxford canals

Fans of Wasps rugby club evidently agree. The bar is abuzz with their discussions before and after matches at their comparatively new home at the nearby Ricoh Arena. And the Greyhound is hardly lacking customers at other times. Maybe that's because of the combination of good ale, good food and the waterside setting.

The bridge across the canal junction was built at the dawn of the Victorian era in 1837. That was at least twelve years after the pub itself, a long, low-roofed and handsome building, bedecked with flower baskets in the summer months when there are plenty of tables twixt building and bankside.

And on chillier days?

Open fires blazed in a bar that would have been full of bargees at one time. A more diverse collection of customers came in more recent times to sit on scrubbed tables packed together on tiled floors strewn with well-worn rugs.

"Great stuff this Bass," claimed one of many vintage adverts around the walls. Sure was, as I recall. Had a similar strength and complexity as Marston's Pedigree with which it shared the bar here as a regular. Both are now brewed by Marston's and both were faultlessly kept when I last called in.

Yet, as I also recall and indeed recorded for readers of *Pint to Pint*, there were some regulars who preferred to savour Theakston's keg mild. They were known as "the Mild Bunch" and they gathered on Friday evenings in the Whippet Bar in what used to be the stables in bargee days.

To quote from what I wrote, "There are a dozen or so men, all in their sixties and seventies, all mild drinkers. All with opinions to air, all ready to break off for a sing-song if and when the ancient piano bursts into life."

The Mild Bunch may well have to book socially distanced tables if and when they sing again as the Whippet Bar and Greyhound Inn are up and running once more.

* * * *

The idea of Bass and Marston's sharing a bar and indeed a brewery would have been unthinkable at one time. Bass has usually been the draught beer of choice among Coventrians of a certain age. But then it has been far more widely available in the city than the ales of its one-time fierce rival.

Closing Time

But in 1923 Marston, Thompson and Evershed, to give them their full title, opened what was evidently seen as something of a local flagship for their products. No expense was spared, it seemed, when it came to building the Biggin Hall on the main Binley Road. A classic example of inter-war mock Tudor, the building was half-timbered with a gabled roof and mullioned windows.

The Biggin Hall

Inside, the expansive lounge bar had a wide open fireplace and a beamed ceiling. Still does. Or at least it did last time I was there in what seems like an eternity ago. We have good friends who live in nearby Stoke Park and Stoke Green and we've been to a few lively evenings upstairs in the function room as well as downstairs.

6 - Batches and Bass in the City of Culture[s]

A large oval table had been a central feature of the lounge for as long as most of us can remember. Seats round there had usually been for long-term regulars who seemed to arrive at a given time as though ready for a board meeting or a four-course meal.

The Biggin was known as the "Banqueting Suite", according to John Middleton, another good friend. John just happened to be in this room watching a "biggish telly" in May, 1987, when Coventry City won a thrilling FA Cup final against Spurs. "I'd stopped smoking but I cracked midway into the second half just after (Keith) Houchen scored to make the score two all. That was my last ciggie ever."

Just as well, perhaps. He would go on to become Professor John Middleton FFPH, FRCP, and currently carries the title "Immediate Past President of the UK Faculty of Public Health".

To us he's better known as "Doctor John", the harmonica-playing half of a folk-blues duo called Doctor Hudson.

Incidentally, the Doc-cum-Prof wrote his first paper for the British Medical Journal in a pub called the New Inn on nearby Bull's Head Lane many years ago. He also wrote "many chapters of a ground-breaking report on The Health of Coventry".

And, yes, it included a chapter on alcohol-related problems .

* * * *

Exactly a century has passed since what you might call "closing time" was called on another landlady known locally as "Ma". Her funeral at Coventry's London Road Cemetery in 1921 was attended by hundreds of mourners.

Like Ma Brown in town at the Old Windmill, Ma Cooper was kindly but stood no nonsense from drunks and potential trouble-makers at the City Arms in Earlsdon. Members of the Royal Munster Fusiliers soon discovered that when they were billeted nearby in 1915. One threatening shout or clench-fisted clout and you'd all too quickly be on your way out.

"She enjoyed a laugh too," according to the Coventry Atlas website. "A letter has recently emerged, written by her in 1915 and recounting her delight in dancing a jig with soldiers."

The City Arms at the heart of Earlsdon

I might add that I'm writing this in a former watch-maker's loft in Earlsdon on St Patrick's Day, 2021. Alas, there'll be no knees-ups in the City Arms or any of the other local pubs or clubs tonight. Thanks to the virus, I've been a mild rover for over a year but I might have a whiskey

6 - Batches and Bass in the City of Culture[s]

as well as a beer while raising a glass to Paddy's night past. Bottled beer, needless to say. Reopening day seems away.

In one of the bedrooms downstairs from my office there's a framed sepia photo of the small and somewhat rustic looking City Arms as it would have been in the days when Mary Jane Cooper, to give Ma her full name, had been persuaded to take on the licence. In 1896, that was, by the Flowers brewing family from twenty miles down the road in Stratford. Mary Jane had been nursemaid to six of their children.

Not too long after her death, the pub was transformed. Or rather knocked down and rebuilt as another mock-Tudor pile. Many years later it would be Wetherspooned.

Plenty of draught beers on offer at reasonable prices and the coffee was good and strong. To buy either you used to have to join an orderly queue along the bar, as though you were at a supermarket till. I always seemed to be behind someone ordering a meal for six with side dishes, several pints from different pumps at either end of the bar. Plus a large glass of red and a regular white wine. Oh yes, and two lattes.

Heaven knows how long the queue might be if and when we can stand at a bar again, maybe two metres apart.

As this book "goes to press" (as we used to say in newspapers) sitting outside licensed premises has been allowed. And rarely does a table stand empty outside the City Arms. The queues are now along the street rather than along the bar. Sunny, shower-free April days have helped, particularly at weekends.

* * * *

Across Earlsdon's main street and a hundred yards or so to the left stands the whitewashed frontage of my beloved local. The Royal Oak was built in 1859 and once had a slaughterhouse at the rear. You could order a pint and a joint. Of raw beef, lamb or pork, that is. Or was.

Closing Time

Among my many fond memories of the Oak over a century and a half later were the pork pies. Although I rarely drink at lunchtimes these days, I used to like calling in around 12.30 on a Sunday for "just the one" lip-smacking pint of Bass and a slice or two of pie, available on every table along with chunks of cheese. All free. You just helped yourself.

That was, needless to say, in those ancient days before the deadly virus spread to these shores. When the Oak did reopen between lockdowns in 2020, you had to sanitise your hands, press your phone to the NHS track-and-trace app, wait to be shown to your pre-booked table and sit at least half a dart's throw away from anyone else.

The Royal Oak before lockdown

6 - Batches and Bass in the City of Culture[s]

Fair enough. The staff had to obey governmental guidance. And the Oak has always offered table service "early doors".

On chilly days the open fireplaces would be glowing on both sides of a bar where scrubbed tables were bordered by wooden settles and plain walls were bedecked with framed sketches and black and white photos.

You could set your watch by the entry of certain regulars. Same time, same seat. "A place for everyone and everyone in their place," to misquote Samuel Smiles.

My good friend Bruce Walker booked a table for April 13, the day after this year's first reopening day. Thankfully, the abattoir was closed down a very long time ago and, believe me, there are far worse places to sit outside these days. Glass panelling had been slotted along the sides of the rear terrace to keep out chilly winds while electric fires glowed down from on high along the back walls.

While savouring a beautifully kept draught bitter draught bitter for the first time in many a month, I found myself gazing wistfully at the glazed exterior of the function room. Many a memory is harboured in there -- from my oldest son-in-law's thirtieth birthday party to suppers, quizzes and poetry nights to raise funds for Earlsdon's wonderful community-run library. Not forgetting rugby afternoons and evenings during the home internationals. With free hot dogs at half time, what's more.

As ever in Coventry, you rarely knew who was English or Welsh, Scottish or Irish. Until kick-off. Thereafter there was much shouting at the screen and celebrating of tries. I once watched the England-Ireland game with a bloke called Pat who turned out to be English and someone else called Pete who all too evidently supported Ireland.

No matter. After the final whistle, we shook hands and had a pint together in a convivial space that I miss almost as much as the main bar.

Closing Time

Mind you, the pub up the road, round the corner and further along Warwick Street once harboured perhaps the most fabled function room in Coventry. That was back in the 1980s during the reign of Wal Haydon and his wife Sheila.

The Earlsdon Cottage in its new format

The Earlsdon Cottage had been converted from a mid-19th century watchmaker's cottage into a public house in 1867. Some one-hundred-and-twenty years later a senior brewery executive revealed that the Cottage sold more Bass than any other outlet in the brewery's considerable estate – apart, that is, from a Black Country pub sited almost next door to a foundry.

6 - Batches and Bass in the City of Culture[s]

Wal was justifiably proud of his Bass and evidently looked on it as a lubricant for the vocal chords. The sizeable function room at the back of the pub staged a "free 'n' easy" sing-along almost every night of the week and he liked to round off the evening with his rendering of *Delilah*.

It's fair to say that he neither looked nor sounded like Tom Jones. Wal's wardrobe of choice was a green cardigan with leather elbow patches and open-toed sandals over grey, woolly socks.

A regular trio performed on Sunday lunchtimes. On the piano was Des Tobin, the genial Irish musician and wit whom we last met in the Black Horse, Spon End. Whatever he played, there was rarely a moment when Des didn't have a smouldering ciggie clamped between his lips.

The smoking ban was still a couple of decades hence, by which time Wal and Sheila had long gone. It's fair to say that the Haydons' haven has been through many manifestations since. Briefly – very briefly – it even harboured a gay bar.

More recently the building was bought up by Wells and Co (formerly Charles Wells) from Bedfordshire. They invested considerable sums in transforming the place, only to see it shut down for many a month, like many another pub.

Before lockdown it offered "artisan pizzas, bubbling pots and vegan delights". Not sure what Wal would have made of that. But he could rest assured that a range of real ales was available in the front bar – the products of Charles Wells, plus one or two "guest beers". No Bass, mind you. That remains part of the past, along with free and easies in a fuggy function room.

Closing Time

Chapter Seven

Cricketing Pubs and the Tales Spun Around Them

Whether you like the game or not, there's no denying that cricket is deeply engrained in the national identity. You only have to look at the number of pubs called the Cricketers or the Cricketers' Arms. Bending arms at the nearest tavern to the ground has been part of the game's traditions for centuries.

Those traditions started in earnest on Broadhalfpenny Down in Hampshire around the middle of the eighteenth century. The licensee of the nearby Bat and Ball, one Richard Nyren, captained the Hambledon village team that beat the All-England XI on no fewer than twenty-nine occasions.

His son John chronicled those games in a book called *The Cricketers of My Time*, extracts from which were framed on one of the pub walls when I called in to do a *Pint to Pint* column some years ago. Having just found the cutting, I see that the taxi driver charged me eighteen quid for the journey from Petersfield Station. *Sunday Telegraph* expenses were generous in those days, bearing in mind the train as well as taxi fare. Not forgetting food and drink.

According to the younger Nyren's reports, the spectators on Broad Halfpenny Down drank barleycorn ale that "flared like turpentine" at 2d a pint while watching the likes of Edward "Lumpy" Stevens bowling crippling underarm "shooters" to pad-less legs. Or William "Silver Billy" Beldham wielding his bat with "a wrist that seemed to turn on springs of the finest steel".

The Fuller's London Pride was somewhat more expensive than the barleycorn on my visit. Didn't flare like turpentine, mind you. But it did sharpen the appetite for a menu that included game when in season. In fact, I fell into conversation with the local gamekeeper. He was sitting at the bar nursing a pint of Gales HSB, having been up long before I'd caught my early-morning train.

Pewter tankards dangled from weathered beams over the bar and horse-brasses glinted around open fires. A classic village pub, then, with a legendary cricket field across the road and a kindly landlord who gave me a lift back to the station at no charge whatsoever.

The Bat and Ball

And now?

According to the Bat and Ball's website, on-line bookings started on April 5, 2021 – a week before opening time. For outside seats only, needless to say. Not a bad view, mind you, particularly for those with a taste for the game. Cricket, that is, rather than pheasant or grouse.

* * * *

7 - Cricketing Pubs and the Tales Spun Around Them

Time for a brief diversion at this point -- to the other end of England and a very different pub in a very different world. The Rohan Kanhai was named after a dashing batsman of my youth. He was part of the West Indies side that came to England in 1963 and turned me on to Test cricket as an impressionable fourteen-year-old glued to my parents' black and white telly.

The Rohan Kanhai inn sign

So why was there a pub named after him in Ashington, Northumberland, once known as the "biggest mining village in the world" and better known for its footballing connections? Birthplace of the Charlton brothers, no less. Yes, Bobby and Jack. Not forgetting their Mum's cousin "Wor" Jackie Milburn of Newcastle United. England players all.

For a West Indian to qualify to play county cricket in England back then he first had to play for a season at club level. Kanhai duly turned out for Ashington CC in the summer of '64. His batting average was

93.62 and, as a result, this famous footballing town won the local league at cricket. "Canny lad and he liked a rum and a game of dominoes," according to one of the club cricketers hereabouts.

The pub named after the "canny" Kanhai was packed when I called in. That may have been because Wetherspoon's were charging just £1.69 for a pint at the time. Cheap even in 2013 when I was researching a book called *Britain's Lost Mines*.

I was waiting to catch the next X22 back to Newcastle from the nearby bus terminus. Plenty of photographs and potted biographies around the pub walls to read in the meantime, including many a tribute to the "canny lad" after whom the pub was named. Yes, I'd paid a small sum for a pint, but my stomach was too full to drink much of it.

One of Ashington's many former miners had shown me round the town's closed pits earlier and given me an insight into its rich seam of history. Then he'd driven me back to his house where his wife had served up an enormous afternoon tea, including bacon-and-egg pie and thickly buttered scones.

Not forgetting ham rolls served up with "pease pudding", an acquired taste and very much a local delicacy. Most unlikely to be served with a game supper at the Bat and Ball in rural Hampshire.

* * * *

Everywhere in England seems a long way from Ashington. Even Scarborough lies over a hundred miles south. Yet I always think of that entertaining seaside town as a long way north when I set off for the annual cricket festival. Not in the summer of 2020, mind you, for obvious reasons.

The year before the pandemic struck I had been carrying out diligent research during the match between Yorkshire and Nottinghamshire for the final chapter of a book called *The Festive Soul of English Cricket*. But I did find time for a lunchtime pint with two old mates from

Nottingham days. One was Allister Craddock, former current affairs producer for ITV, whom we met in Chapter Five. The other was Pete Dredge, freelance cartoonist for many a national publication, who now lives in Scarborough with his wife Sharon.

Maybe it was Pete's local knowledge that led us a short distance from the ground to a pub called The Albert, sited a bit further along the North Marine Road and serving the best pint of Tetley's that I'd savoured for some years. "Born in Leeds," said a sign near a handpump that gave it a suitably creamy head. "No longer made there," it could have added, but didn't.

A nearby wall was covered with images and information about past matches at the nearby cricket ground, a bewitching mixture of the scenic and the homely. But eventually we moved to a table outside and fell into conversation with a retired finance director from Huddersfield who was soon reminiscing about a childhood trip to see Don Bradman's Australians at a packed Headingley.

Back to Leeds again.

Not for too long, however. A passing seagull chose to open its bowels over our table as if to comment on Nottinghamshire's chances of saving the current match. Perhaps it was time to get back to the ground down the road.

* * * *

My other regular festival visits include Chesterfield and Cheltenham, two towns with very little in common apart from the first three letters of their names. I have fond memories of both and, as usual, those memories include visits to characterful pubs close by those distinctive grounds.

By 2019 the Royal Oak in Chesterfield had changed a bit since my first lunchtime visit six summers previously. But it still stood proudly in the narrow byways of The Shambles, its top-floor timbers on the outside as skew-whiff as the nearby crooked spire. Well, the building dated back to the twelfth century in parts.

The Royal Oak in Chesterfield

The beams in the "best room", its vaulted ceiling illuminated by slits of stained glass, were almost certainly not original. No matter. It felt good to be there on a sweltering day in 2013 listening to Yorkshiremen discussing the morning's play at Queen's Park during which their "lads" had dominated Derbyshire, the "home" side.

Licensee John (no, not "Johnnie") Walker came from Scarborough and briefly raised hopes among his fellow county-men by fastening on a pump clip advertising Black Sheep bitter from north Yorks. Then he pulled a sample, held it up to the light and proclaimed, "Not right yet."

7 - Cricketing Pubs and the Tales Spun Around Them

Can't pretend that I cared too much, having sampled the first swig of a rare treat. No wonder Courage Directors was originally confined to the brewery directors' dining rooms. It was all too obviously their finest bitter and too evidently better than their "Best". Particularly when it was kept in such perfect condition as it was on that summer lunchtime in Chesterfield.

It went down a treat with the scampi and chips. Not just any scampi but "Whitby" scampi – "plump and breadcrumbed and infinitely preferable to those rubbery shreds that used to come in a basket, encased by batter that deflated with an audible hiss when prodded with a fork," as I reminisced with *Telegraph* readers of *Pint to Pint*. Many of them, I suspected, would be old enough to remember the days when "scampi in the basket", forced down with Watney's Red Barrel or Whitbread Tankard, was considered the height of sophistication.

* * * *

Talking of sophistication, perhaps it's time to move on to Cheltenham, another fine setting to watch the red-ball game on festival week. Gloucestershire had first pitched up here in 1872 when one WG Grace triumphed with ball rather than bat in hand. Took twelve wickets for sixty-three, in case you're interested, and scored the first triple century in a county match three years later. Against Yorkshire, would you believe?

Okay, okay. Enough of cricket. "What about the 'boozer'?" to use a term rarely heard in Cheltenham.

Well, it just so happens that the walk back to the station from the College Ground is a lengthy one. Luckily, I spotted a good place to break the journey after watching a day's play against Worcestershire in 2019.

Sited at one end of the chic Cheltenham terrace of Montpellier Villas, the pub could best be described as "shabby-chic". In fact, that's how I later described it in *Pint to Pint*.

Beyond the handsomely engraved windows were well-worn seats and tables. A slumbering Labrador was sprawled across a corner of evidently well-trodden floorboards. "Watch this," said one of the regulars. He then plucked a dog-biscuit from a jar on the bar and tossed it over his shoulder. The Labrador leapt to life and caught it in his chops as instinctively as former Gloucestershire and England wicketkeeper Jack Russell would once have pouched a cricket ball in his gloves.

The dog-biscuit trick had evidently been done at regular intervals judging by the lack of reaction from two nearby crib players. They were sitting at a well-scrubbed table close to the sizeable "Snug" with an open fire and book cases crammed with old-fashioned board games such as Monopoly and Cluedo. Plenty of second-hand books as well, including the Good Beer Guide for 2003.

A reminder there that it was time to choose from one of the regular bitters among the ever-changing guest beers. A Yorkshire beer, as it happened. No, not Black Sheep but Timothy Taylor's Landlord.

Went down a treat and, once it had been seen off, I almost tripped rather than trudged to the station.

* * * *

Two more treks from trains to grounds come to mind. Arundel Station stands in rural Sussex, just twenty-three miles from Brighton where I usually stay overnight at the family home of our middle daughter, Suzi. Yet the journey to Arundel takes an hour and a half, via two trundling trains. Then you have to walk about a mile and a half.

Is it worth is?

You bet it is.

One of the most beautiful settings for county cricket in all England lies within the turrets of Arundel Castle. Sussex CCC have paid an annual visit for many a year, with the exception of 2020. You can see those turrets getting closer as you pace past fields full of June blooms and,

7 - Cricketing Pubs and the Tales Spun Around Them

closer still, as you cross the river and catch sight of the handsome frontage of the White Hart.

A good place to beak the journey back to the station come close of play?

You bet it is. Or rather "was" and, hopefully, will be again.

Scrubbed tables and wooden settles used to be packed with parties of cricket lovers discussing the day's play and much else. Behind the central fireplace was a cosy, snug-like seating area. And decorative Harvey's mirrors reflected the general bonhomie.

Was the Sussex Best as good as it could be?

You bet it was. And will be again, I'm sure. Well, as sure as I can be.

* * * *

The lengthy walk from Worcester's Foregate Street Station to New Road, home of Worcestershire's county ground, was also well worth it. And I speak as a man of neighbouring Warwickshire.

Just as worthwhile was the shorter lunchtime stroll back across the Severn Bridge, along the opposite bank for a hundred yards or so and through the grounds of Worcester College. Over a busy main road and slightly to the right is the corner of Fish Street where stands a splendidly eccentric source of refreshment.

I've been a man of the Plough since I stumbled across it by chance after a slightly boring morning's play on the other side of the river. A bar lined with beer and "local" cider pumps stood atop steps in a handsomely tiled passageway.

Stalwartly pulling those pumps during my last visit two summers ago was a Polish woman who may have been slightly baffled by conversations about cricket that seemed to resound around the passageway as discerning locals and visiting supporters piled in.

Any statistical disputes could be resolved by consulting one of a selection of Wisden almanacs dating back to 1940 and lining the windowsill in the room to the left. Plenty of reference books on the mantelpiece in there as well. Never mind Google: there were the facts in black and white beneath a small glass case containing a framed bottle of Worcestershire sauce.

Bottles of a different kind lined the shelves running around the upper levels of the room across the passageway. An abundance of whisky up there included at least "30 single malts", according to a chalked sign on a blackboard outside the pub.

I stuck to a single pint of Hobson's from neighbouring Shropshire. Yes, it was tip-top but, no, I didn't want to miss the afternoon's play or, indeed, a cup of tea and a slice of cake at the Ladies' Pavilion. The ladies did us gents proud, as usual.

And, hopefully, there won't be too many changes at the Plough post-lockdown. Pre-booking tables and attaching phone apps doesn't quite fit its timeless image. All I can hope at this stage is that it will have reopened come the hour, come the day of my next visit to New Road.

* * * *

Time, perhaps, to sail across the Midlands from the Severn to the Trent. Yes, back to Nottingham. Well, Trent Bridge is a Test ground with a rich history. And next door stands the Trent Bridge Inn, built in 1890 in sturdy red brick with a proudly jutting frontage. After its takeover by Wetherspoon's in 2011, it became a gallery for many an evocative photograph of Nottinghamshire players past.

If memory serves, that Retford ragamuffin Derek Randall was pictured in baggy shorts and pulled-up school socks in one photo, wielding the bat with which he scored his unforgettable 174 for England in Melbourne in another. The great Gary . . . sorry, Sir Garfield Sobers, was somewhat bafflingly tucked away on a wall near the gents. But the

7 - Cricketing Pubs and the Tales Spun Around Them

former West Indies and Notts all-rounder was launching into a characteristically dashing drive.

The Trent Bridge Inn

Local legends from other eras were on other walls. Here Harold Larwood and Bill Voce from pre-war summers when Notts was a "miner" county packed with players from the pits; there a dynasty of Gunns, headed by William (1858-1921) who played for England at football as well as cricket and went on to co-found the sports shop Gunn and Moore.

Across the way was George Parr (1826-'91) who hit so many sixes into the branches of a Trent Bridge tree at square leg that it became known as Parr's tree. Until, that is, it was blown down during a storm in 1976. I remember looking at the Parr's sepia portrait and wondering how that mighty smiter managed to clout so many sixes with a bat that hardly looked capable of propelling the ball as far as the square-leg umpire.

The camera was in its infancy back in the days of William Clarke (1798-1856). That may explain why such a significant figure in the history of English cricket was framed at the centre of a painting of the All-England XI in the pub's function room.

Well, it was Clarke who founded the All-England XI in 1846. And it was Clarke who, a few years earlier, had organised the laying out of the Trent Bridge ground soon after laying the landlady of the tavern that once stood on the site of its late-Victorian replacement.

Her name was Mary Chapman and she kicked him out not too long after their marriage in 1837. Bit of a lad was "Clarkey". In the painting he's sporting a top hat and pulling up his trousers over a substantial stomach. Apparently he had nothing more than a cigar and a glass of soda water for lunch but a whole goose for his supper. Washed down, needless to say, with beverages somewhat stronger than soda water.

The TBI had become my favourite Wetherspoon's venue long before lockdown. Not on Test Match days, however, when it tended to be rammed to the rafters. As for the pub called the Test Match, that has long stood a mile or so down the road from the ground – a bit of a hike during the lunch interval if you didn't want to miss much of the afternoon's play. Well worth a visit at other times, mind you.

Last time I was there the entrance to that Grade II*-listed Art Deco palace of a pub was via a revolving door reminiscent of Odeon cinemas past. Inside was wood panelling inset with imposingly mounted images of larger-than-life local cricketers from the century before last. Chief among them were Clarke and Parr, early stars in the rich historic tapestry of Trent Bridge.

I have tickets for two days of the forthcoming Test Match there against India in August, 2021. One day will be with old friends from Nottingham, another with good mates from Coventry. And, yes, there could be a pint or two at lunchtime and after close of play.

7 - Cricketing Pubs and the Tales Spun Around Them

Sharing convivial times with friends is part of what pubs are about. Making new friends or acquaintances, too, be they sitting at nearby tables or standing at the bar. If and when we're allowed to, that is.

As this book goes to press, the lifting of all restrictions is still a while away. Meanwhile, a new wave of the virus rampages across India and new strains keep putting up new challenges to the much celebrated vaccine roll-out on this side of the Channel.

These uncertainties may be part of the past in the not too distant future. Hope so. I also hope that the majority of pubs that we've visited in this and preceding chapters will have reopened. Whether they can stay open is another matter. Lost profits have to be re-made and debts repaid. Not easy if – and it's still an "if" – social distancing cannot safely be discarded. Not easy if so-called vaccine passports are ever required just to step over the threshold. Admittedly that's a big "if".

There are many more "ifs" and "buts" at this stage. What does seem likely is that even more of the characterful inns that we cherish will be calling a permanent closing time.

Closing Time

Some of the many photos of Notts cricketers past ranged around the walls of the Trent Bridge Inn

Gary Sobers in characteristically flamboyant style

Harold Larwood unleashing a fearsome fast one

Derek Randall, the Retford ragamuffin

George Parr, the mighty smiter who had a Trent Bridge tree named after him

WG Grace's last appearance at Trent Bridge in June 1989

(Pictures courtesy of Wetherspoons)

BIOGRAPHY

Chris Arnot has written thirteen non-fiction books. *Small Island by Little Train* was published by the AA in 2017 and shortlisted for the Edward Stanford awards for travel writing the following year. Marcus Beckmann called it "very much a state-of-the nation book" in his *Daily Mail* review.

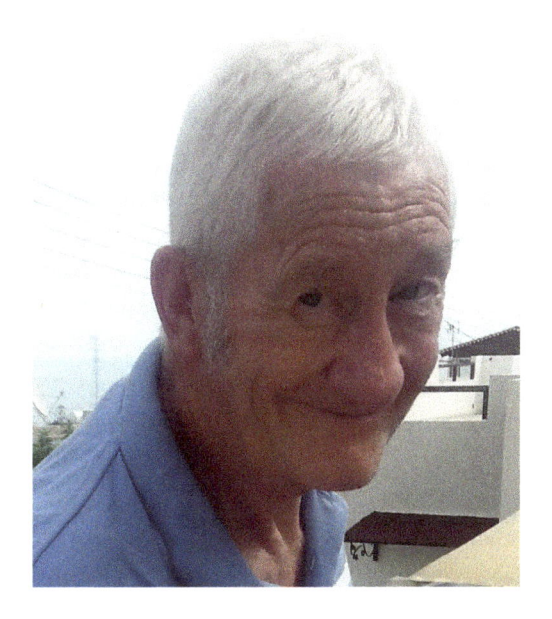

Chris also wrote four of the *Britain's Lost* series for Aurum. Britain's Lost Cricket Grounds was reprinted twice after some glowing reviews. The late Frank Keating described it as "a coffee-table classic for and of posterity" in the *Guardian* and Jim Holden hailed it as "the best sports book of 2011" in the *Sunday Express*. Billy Elliot creator Lee Hall called Britain's Lost Mines as "an extraordinary gallery of lives and landscapes".

As a national freelance journalist for a quarter of a century or so, Chris wrote for the *Guardian*, the Independent, the *Observer*, the *Times* and the *Telegraph*. And, until lockdown, he was a regular contributor to the *Sunday Telegraph*'s Pint to Pint column, a collection of which was published in 2016.

Closing Time

BIBLIOGRAPHY

The Telegraph Pint to Pint: a crawl around Britain's best pubs
(Icon Books, 2016)

A Thousand Years of Coventry Pubs
By John Ashby, Fred Luckett and David McGory
(TW Printing, 2014)

The Good Beer Guide, 2021
(Camra Books, 2020)

Also:

Britain's Lost Breweries and Beers
(Aurum Press, 2012)

Britain's Lost Mines
(Aurum Press, 2013)

Small Island by Little Train
(AA Publishing, 2017)

and

The Festive Soul of English Cricket
(Takahe Publishing, 2019)

    …. all by Chris Arnot

Closing Time